MISSION SAUDI

Aloke Lal is a former Indian Police Service (IPS) officer and best-selling author. During his thirty-seven years in the khaki, he helmed several challenging assignments in the crime-infested belts of the Hindi heartland, coming face to face with criminals ranging from drug lords to feared militants. Post-retirement, he took to writing in the long form with his debut book *The Barabanki Narcos: Busting India's Most Notorious Drug Cartel*, which is now being adapted into a web series. He has co-authored four more true-crime books since. Aloke was felicitated twice by the President of India: for 'Long and Meritorious Services' and for 'Distinguished Services'. An accomplished painter, Lal is the Festival Director of the Crime Literature Festival of India. He has been a quizmaster on Doordarshan and is also a TEDx speaker.

Maanas Lal is the co-author of four acclaimed true-crime books—*Murder in the Bylanes*, *On the Trail of Thugs, Fangs of Death* and *Codename Stallion*—and has penned hundreds of incisive columns for leading publications. A software engineer, he fuses technology with creativity, pioneering a unique digital painting style collected worldwide. A musician who travels the world with a six-string on his back, Maanas has starred in viral music videos. He loves teaching, and his soft-skills workshops are a regular feature at some of India's leading schools and professional institutions. Frequently seen on television debates on issues ranging from climate change to gender inclusivity, Maanas is a state-level sportsperson and award-winning cultural voice. A TEDx speaker, he also curates the Crime Literature Festival of India.

MISSION SAUDI

Based on India's First Extradition of a Sexual Predator

ALOKE LAL
MAANAS LAL

RUPA

Published by
Rupa Publications India Pvt. Ltd 2025
161-B/4, Gulmohar House,
Yusuf Sarai Community Centre,
New Delhi 110049

Sales centres:
Bengaluru Chennai
Hyderabad Kolkata Mumbai

For reasons of prudence and as a mark of respect to the victim's family, the names of some characters in the book have been replaced with aliases.

The book is based on the judgement of the trial court, police station records and conversations with Merin Joseph, the victim's family and other sources. Some elements in the story have been dramatized. This narrative is not intended to in any way influence judicial process.

P-ISBN: 978-93-7003-354-2
E-ISBN: 978-93-7003-376-4

First impression 2025

10 9 8 7 6 5 4 3 2 1

Printed in India

Contents

Contents

Authors' Note

The feat of effecting the first extradition of a rape accused to bring him to face trial in India from the Kingdom of Saudi Arabia had caught unprecedented public imagination after the media prominently reported it in 2019. Merin Joseph, the young Commissioner of Police, who led this process, became an overnight celebrity. The media said a lot, but a lot more needed to be told. While the accomplishment itself makes for a compelling story, it was preceded by the making of an IPS officer—the long hours she had spent preparing to compete with the best in the country, the sweat and blood shed during a taxing period of tough physical and mental training, and the rough and tumble of the life of a law-keeper. There was also something to be said about her team from Kerala Police and members of other agencies that made the extradition possible. *Mission Saudi* attempts to convey the suffering of the victim, and of her family. There is a measured sprinkling of fiction at some points in the book to fill in blanks and make the narrative more reader-friendly.

Prologue

Onam celebrations were in full swing in Kerala. The homecoming of King Mahabali was being marked with the usual fervour in the Laksham Veedu[1] colony of Clappana village in Kollam district. It was the Chathayam day—the birthday of Narayana Guru, the nineteenth-century saint and social reformer who fought against the caste system. This day—a public holiday in the state of Kerala—is marked by processions, conferences, floral tributes, community prayers and feasts, and feeding the poor.

Upasana had been preparing for her dance performance for weeks. The Kathakali dances performed around Onam are watched by huge crowds and Upasana wanted to put her best foot forward. Both her parents, Geetha and Vinaykumar, and her stepfather Gopikumar, whom she endearingly called Pappa, were there to cheer her on. By her side, as always, was Pooja, her elder sister. The girls were keenly observing the festivities in the city centre. The whole of Clappana village was going to view

[1]Aimed at providing housing for the underprivileged.

Upasana's maiden Onam performance and Pooja was the one calming her nerves.

Hours before the staging, the sisters made their way back home through palm trees for a final dress rehearsal. Their home was named Pooja-Shraddha after the two elder sisters. Upasana was the youngest of the three siblings. The family had close relatives visiting, as was customary for that time of the year. Everyone applauded once Upasana was done with her rehearsal. Her movements were full of grace and genuine reverence for the classical dance form. Upasana looked at her elder sister for a final nod of approval which she promptly got. Pooja was evidently proud of her sister's dancing prowess.

'You look beautiful in this attire,' Pooja told Upasana as she helped her dress up.

'Thank you, Didi. What would I do without you!' Upasana exclaimed.

'Nothing. I am your Mahabali.'

Both sisters burst into laughter. This was followed by a warm embrace.

Once Upasana was done with her make-up, Pooja went to the washroom located just outside the main house to touch up her kajal. She wielded the kajal pencil with remarkable dexterity. For a student of Class 9, her creative talents were well-honed and her future in the arts looked promising. Pooja looked at the mirror after the kajal was in place and could not help but admire the way the make-up highlighted her dark-brown irises.

Satisfied with her look for the evening, Pooja unbolted

the door and stepped out only to be shadowed by an imposing human figure. Before she could wriggle out of the narrow space between her and the person, her arms were pinned to the door.

Pooja went numb. She felt ice-cold lips against her face. A few wet kisses were landed on her blouse too. She tried to shout but a hand covered her mouth. She managed to stamp the molester on the toes and ran as fast as she could. As she turned into her home, she saw festive faces all around. She was shaking and too flustered to speak. The others were preoccupied with the décor and Pooja did not want to confide in Upasana who was slated to perform soon.

The unmistakable shadow of Pooja's tormentor flanked hers as she stared helplessly at the ground. She turned around to see the face of her father's friend, one that she had adored all her life. It was a stake through her heart, a betrayal of the worst kind, a picture of unfathomable depravity!

Uncomfortable Truths

Pooja was seated in a corner of the library at the Sree Vivekananda Higher Secondary School in Clappana. This corner of the room held some of her fondest memories. With more than four thousand books available to read, this haven of knowledge had shaped Pooja's ideological make-up. She had learnt concepts ranging from simple grammar to complex theoretical physics in this very room. She had also found quiet, and occasional peace, amidst the books. The library opened into the central yard of the school, which had two large trees. Pooja loved to observe nesting birds from the library. She had seen eggs hatch and chicks come to life for the first time from where she was seated. Yet, today the library felt like a black hole which had consumed her. Her feet were numb and she could barely move a muscle. She clutched onto her belly which hurt like a thousand bee stings. Pooja was staring at her examination papers which were swarming with red marks. She had never performed so poorly. This result was a shock not just to her but also to her teachers and classmates.

Just then, Ammu, Pooja's closest friend, tapped her on the shoulder. Ammu was the only one who knew why Pooja was in an extremely depressed state of mind. After seeing her results, Ammu realized that continuing to harbour Pooja's secret would be to her detriment.

'Pooja, we have to tell Geetha Aunty about what you have been through. You must not continue to be miserable.' Ammu looked at Pooja, who was staring at her mark sheet in disbelief, as if the marks would magically change into better news.

'I can't tell her, Ammu. She will die… Amma will die.' Pooja mumbled.

'But what about you? You are dying within.'

'No, Ammu. Imagine the impact it will have on *Achan*[1]. Pappa will also be devastated. They can never imagine Uncle Satheesh…' Pooja completely broke down while talking.

'You are living a life worse than death. You can't keep this from your family. Let's go and talk to Manju Ma'am. She has always been your favourite.'

Pooja nodded in the negative while grasping her tummy.

'Is the pain back again?'

Pooja winced in extreme discomfort.

'That's it. I am calling Manju Ma'am here. I can't see you like this.'

'No, Ammu. Please don't. If you say anything, I will commit suicide. Please…'

---

[1]Father in Malayalam.

Ammu started sobbing while holding on to her friend's belly. She felt helpless but Pooja's threat to take her own life made her give up the idea of breaking her silence.

Later that evening, Ammu confided in her mother about Pooja's mental state and the horror she had lived through. Ammu's mother asked her to invite Pooja over to their house at the soonest. The next day, Pooja visited them and Ammu's mother convinced her to talk to her teacher about the harassment she had faced. After much persuasion, Pooja agreed.

Manju, Pooja's class teacher, had always been fond of her. Pooja's abysmal performance in the examination had her concerned. When Ammu approached her to have a word with Pooja, she felt relieved. She wanted to know for a while what had been troubling the young girl's heart.

Pooja had spent the morning staring into the well on the school campus. She had brushed aside the thought of jumping into it several times. When Ammu told her that Manju was waiting for her in an empty staff room, Pooja looked into the well one final time. The lifelessness in Pooja's expression startled Ammu, who immediately pulled her away.

'What are you doing?'

'My life is over. I want to disappear.'

'No, Pooja. Please don't say that. Let us please go to Manju Ma'am.'

'I will not be able to look her in the eye. I am dirty.'

'Don't be silly. You are the most beautiful girl I have ever known. Please try and calm the storm within you.'

Ammu put her arms around her friend and they slowly began to walk towards the staff room. As the girls entered the room, Manju was already waiting with a comforting expression. She signalled Ammu to make Pooja sit on a chair opposite her. Manju noticed that as Pooja sat, she held her belly tightly.

'Do you have pain there?' Manju asked Pooja.

Pooja nodded and began to sob.

'What happened? Why is my favourite student in this frame of mind?'

Pooja continued sobbing.

'Consider me like your mother. Is everything okay?'

'Ma'am…'

'Yes, child. You can trust me.'

'Ma'am… I hit myself.'

'Yourself? How?' Manju was taken aback.

'Ma'am, I hit myself with a water bottle.'

'When did this happen?'

'It has been a while. I just had to do it.'

'What reason could you possibly have to hurt yourself?'

'I had to kill it, Ma'am. I am a murderer.' Pooja completely broke down.

Manju was shocked beyond words. She understood that the conversation ahead was way more serious than low marks in an examination.

'You are a wonderful young lady. You are no murderer. What do you mean by "kill it"?'

Pooja was now crying inconsolably. Ammu was making an unsuccessful attempt at calming her.

'Pooja, please talk to me. We are here for you.'

'I killed my…'

'Go on, child.'

'I killed…'

'Pooja…'

'…my baby.' Pooja mumbled.

'I killed my baby.' Pooja said in a stronger tone.

'I killed my baby.' Pooja repeated, this time shouting and wailing.

Both Ammu and Manju held her from either side of the chair. Manju had a look of horror in her eyes. She could hardly believe what she had just heard.

'Your baby? Are you…were you…pregnant?' Manju asked.

Pooja managed to nod in the affirmative.

Manju knew that whatever Pooja had been through was beyond her worst fears. She told Ammu to shut the door of the staff room and get a glass of water for her friend.

'How bad is the pain?'

'I can't bear it anymore.' Pooja sounded spent.

'Let us get you to a doctor.'

'No, Ma'am. My parents will come to know.'

'Has there been any problem other than the pain?'

Pooja looked down. She sank between her shoulders.

Ammu came back to the room with a jar of water. Seeing the shift in Pooja's demeanour, Manju offered her a glass.

'Drink. This will help.'

Pooja drank the water in quick gulps. It looked as though her throat had been dry for days.

'Tell me. Anything other than the pain?'

'Ma'am, I have been bleeding down there.' Pooja began to sob again, muffling clarity from the tail end of the statement.

Manju was stunned into silence.

Five minutes went by without a word spoken.

'Do you want to take a break?' This question was as much for Manju's peace of mind as it was for Pooja's.

Pooja refused this offer. She knew that it would be impossible for her to start talking again. It was now or never.

Manju managed to gather her thoughts quickly and asked, 'When did all this begin?'

'It was Onam…two years ago.'

'What happened then?'

Pooja stared at the door of the staff room. Manju understood that Pooja wanted absolute privacy. She requested Ammu to bolt the door.

'It is just us, Pooja. This is a safe space.'

'Ma'am, he came into the bathroom. I was helpless.'

'Who?' Manju asked instinctively while processing the weight of what Pooja's previous statement implied.

'Achan trusted him like a brother. Pappa too. They both will die.'

Manju held her silence but could not hold back a look of fear in her eyes.

'Ma'am, you will also hate me. Everybody will. I can't...'

'Pooja, you have nothing to worry. I will never give up on you. I promise. Please tell me what happened.'

'He...' Pooja took a gulp. 'Uncle Satheesh...he cornered me the moment I stepped out of the bathroom.'

Manju could hardly believe what she was hearing. Her student's plight was difficult to swallow. A part of her hoped that she would suddenly wake up from this nightmare. Convincing herself that this was indeed real by feeling her knees, she asked, 'Your Uncle?'

'Yes, Ma'am. He pinned me against the door and...'

Manju could see that Pooja was short of breath. She offered her another glass of water which Pooja drank promptly.

'He touched me...it felt like he touched me everywhere.'

Pooja's emotions had been bottled up for far too long. She continued to talk before Manju had fully taken in the gravity of what she was hearing.

'He pushed me against the door and started kissing me. He put his fingers in my mouth, and I couldn't speak. No matter how many times I rinse my mouth, that metallic taste just does not go off my tongue,' Pooja coughed as her taste buds reminded her of that fateful evening and reached for her belly right after.

Manju was teary-eyed. She cleared her throat and said, 'Pooja, I am so proud of you for telling me this. None of this is your fault.'

'Ma'am, he brushed against me and kissed me on the face and then here,' Pooja pointed towards the middle of her chest as she spoke. She then frantically rubbed her face as if trying to remove the sensation of the kisses before adding, 'I stamped him on the foot and somehow escaped the bathroom.'

'Then?' Manju said in a feeble tone.

'It was such a festive ambience outside. I felt like the bright lights around were mocking me. He followed me out soon after and walked with a slight limp. I was too scared to say anything. He just walked past me with a foreboding glance.'

'Did you tell anyone?'

'I wanted to. I really wanted to. After Uncle Satheesh left the house, Upasana and I returned to the Onam celebrations in the colony. She had to give a dance performance, and I did not want to trouble her. I saw Kaladevi *Ammayi*[2] there and immediately went to her.'

'Did you tell her?'

'I tried but all I managed was, "Is Uncle Satheesh a man of good character?"'

'What did your Ammayi say?'

'She said that it was a time of celebration and advised me to not bother about these things. She did not give any real importance to my enquiry and wanted me to enjoy Upasana's performance. After that, whatever little courage I had left to talk also dwindled. I just could not get Uncle

---

[2]Father's sister in Malayalam.

Satheesh's expression out of my head. I was so scared.'

'So you decided to keep all this to yourself?' Manju asked Pooja in stupefaction.

'I thought nobody would believe me. I didn't even tell Ammu till the next time…' Pooja started sobbing again.

'Next time? When?' While Manju had understood that there must be more to Pooja's suffering, she was hoping against hope that there was only one incident of depravity.

As Pooja began to talk further, Manju knew that she would have to bring Pooja's mother into the picture. There was no way that she could be kept in the dark about the burden her daughter had been carrying for nearly two years.

A Thousand Tears

Pooja-Shraddha was freshly bathed in rain. A downpour in January was rare but certainly not unwelcome. With the temperature in the mid-twenties, Geetha was contemplating a walk through the neighbouring paddy fields when her mobile rang. She usually avoided taking calls from numbers which were not in her contact list but something made her pick this one up.

'Geetha Ji, this is Manju. I am Pooja's class teacher.'

'Hello, Manju Ma'am. Of course, Pooja speaks very highly of you. I was expecting a call from the school. Her results are…'

'This is not about her results. She has severe pain in her stomach. Can you please come to the school?'

The wet floor of the veranda suddenly felt more slippery to Geetha as she tried to take a seat, 'Is it that serious? She was holding her belly the other day too but I didn't think much of it. I will come at once.'

Geetha immediately made her way to the Sree Vivekananda Higher Secondary School. The guard had already been sounded about her arrival and immediately took her to the staff room where Pooja, Ammu, Manju and the Principal of the school, Sheeja, were waiting for her.

Pooja was staring at the ground. As Geetha held her hand, she broke down.

'What happened, sweetheart?' Geetha sounded anxious. She had never known Pooja to be a crier.

'Ma'am, she has been through a lot in the last couple of years. The issue is very serious and that is why as a matter of protocol, I have requested Principal Ma'am to be here too.'

Manju went on to explain the first episode of harassment that Pooja had faced at the hands of Thakshak Satheesh during the Onam celebrations at Veedu Laksham colony. By the time she finished, Geetha was sitting on the floor wrapped around her daughter's feet in extreme guilt. She had known Satheesh for decades. He was a close friend of Gopikumar and later grew close to the whole family.

'*Beta* (Child), you should have told me…' Geetha kept saying over and over again.

Just as Manju was about to move on to the second incident, Pooja spoke, 'Amma, please don't tell Achan or Pappa… Amma please.'

Geetha hugged her daughter in response. While in her mother's arms, Pooja said, 'Amma, Uncle Satheesh had the audacity to come after me in Sooryabhavanam too.'

This came as a shock to Geetha. Sooryabhavanam was her mother-in-law's home where Satheesh and her husband, Vinaykumar, had originally forged a strong friendship. Such was their equation that their daughters had always treated Satheesh like an uncle, their father's real brother. To imagine him resorting to such depravity in a home which had given him refuge through his toughest times made Geetha feel sick in the stomach.

'Tell me about it, Beta?' An evidently crestfallen Geetha managed to ask.

'I was alone in the house, dusting the tables and chairs when he came from behind…' Pooja started wailing.

Manju stepped in and spoke to Pooja, 'You have been so brave. Please talk to Geetha Ji. She will understand.'

'…and he took off my dupatta. I tried to run away but he just won't let go. He pulled my legs and I fell to the ground. Then he tied my legs with the dupatta.' Pooja scurried through her statement just to lessen the hurt of thinking back to her ordeal.

She gathered herself once more and continued, 'Then he…' Pooja swallowed a gulp of tears, '…he tore my blouse with his bare hands. I still remember the sound of the fabric falling apart. I felt the pain of every thread. He tied my hands with what was left of the blouse.'

Only Geetha knew what she was going through while listening to Pooja. A daughter she had raised with immense protection even through financial hardships had been treated like a commodity to be abused by a person her husband considered a brother.

'Once again, Uncle Satheesh…he kissed me on the lips and the chest. And then he squeezed me tight, so tight that my ribs crackled. I managed to push him away and shouted incessantly. Perhaps the fear of getting caught made him stop and he suddenly ran away.'

'When did this happen?' Geetha tried to sound composed.

'This was also in August, Amma. Soon after the first incident.'

'Beta, you should have told me…' Geetha said once more.

'I was so ashamed of myself…' Just as Pooja had started to open up to her mother, the pain in her belly hurt like a jellyfish sting. She fell to the ground. Manju and Ammu immediately helped her up while Geetha hugged her and cried.

'Why does it hurt so much?' Geetha asked looking at her daughter's belly, 'Is there more to what Satheesh did?' Geetha was fearing the worst.

Pooja looked at her belly and then at her mother, 'Amma… I killed it.'

Unwilling to register what Pooja's eye movements indicated, Geetha said, 'No. Pooja, there has to be a mistake. He didn't…'

Geetha's statement was interrupted by Pooja's anguished shriek. She collapsed to the ground again.

Seeing Pooja's plight and the gravity of the situation, Manju gestured to Ammu to leave. The young girl reluctantly left the side of her best friend.

Manju looked at Geetha, 'Ma'am, there was one more incident.'

Geetha went pale. She folded her hands as if to request Manju to stop.

'We must contact the Child Welfare Committee. They will know what to do.' Manju told Geetha.

Geetha nodded while wearing a look of utter helplessness.

'No, I want Amma to know. She must know.' Pooja said in a rather assertive tone, picking herself up and sitting back on the chair.

'What?' Geetha mumbled looking straight into Pooja's eyes.

'The third time was also in Sooryabhavanam.'

Geetha remained mum but her eyes asked the question for her, 'When?'

'Amma, this was in April last year. I thought he had given up on harassing me after the long gap but I was wrong. You are right, I should have told you.' Pooja sobbed.

'I was reading the newspaper in the hall. Once again, he came from behind me.' Pooja started moving her shoulders in discomfort as she spoke.

Geetha thought of her husband. She could not bring herself to even imagine the impact all this would have on him. Seeing the anxiousness on her mother's face, Pooja said, 'Amma… I am so sorry. I am so…so sorry.'

'It's not your place to be sorry, Pooja. I should have understood what you were going through. I have failed as a mother.'

'No, Amma. I made every effort to hide my strife from all of you. It is not your fault.'

Manju thought that Geetha must be privy to every detail of the third incident. She looked at Pooja and said, 'Please tell Geetha Ji the rest of what he did.'

Pooja looked at her mother and began to sob.

'Tell me, Pooja. Manju Ma'am is right.' Geetha said.

'Amma…this time he just did not stop. He…he… he raped me.'

Geetha looked like her soul had left her body. Her expression became death-like. She could not find it in her to express what she felt. The tears just fell without as much as a twitch of any other muscle.

'Amma…he dragged me to the bedroom. My head hit the wardrobe as he was pulling me across the floor. Everything after that feels like a blur, an eerily vivid blur. I felt him tearing my clothes apart and inserting them in my mouth. I tried to shout but…but… I just couldn't.'

Geetha continued to listen in stunned silence.

'Amma, I knew that Uncle Satheesh would eventually leave for Saudi and nothing would happen even if I complained. I did not want the whole family to become a laughing stock for the village.'

'None of this matters, Pooja. I care about you, not about what the villagers say.'

'Amma… I was so lost. I unburdened myself on Ammu but made her swear not to tell anyone. I was particularly scared because…'

Geetha and Manju exchanged a glance. Manju looked ready to console Geetha.

'...I was pregnant. I had missed my period. I took a test and...'

'O my little girl!' Geetha wailed.

'Amma...' Pooja wailed too.

'But Amma, you needn't worry. I killed it.'

'Killed what? How? Why?' Questions flooded Geetha's mind.

'I... I jammed my water bottle into my belly with all the force I had. I thought of how Achan and Pappa would feel if they came to know and that gave me strength.'

For the next several minutes, there was pin-drop silence. It was broken when a peon walked in with the message that a van had been arranged to take Pooja to the office of the Child Welfare Committee.

Only a day later, Pooja was on her way to Mahilamandiram, a shelter home, after a session of counselling at the Child Welfare Committee. Geetha, who accompanied her to the rescue home, could hardly recognize her stone-faced daughter. As the van carrying them drove over the Setu Lakshmi Bayi, Pooja saw the Arabian Sea. She loved when the sea would swell after a spell of rain but today the waves looked like they would consume her. She clutched onto Geetha every time she saw her beloved sea on the hour-long journey.

Jijimol, the Circle Officer (CO) attached to the Women's Cell, had several letters sitting on her desk as usual. However, this one from the Child Welfare Committee caught her eye first. As she read through its contents and got a summary of what Pooja had gone through, her emotions got the better of her and she pounded both her hands on the table in front. Her confidential assistant quickly made his way to the room to see what the commotion was about. She quickly helped herself to a glass of water and made haste to get to Mahilamandiram. On the way, she asked for Constable Renjini, who was on emergency duty at the Oachira police station, to be assigned to the case. As Renjini was being filled in by her superior on the details of the crime, she looked out of her office window at the Parabrahma Temple. It was the time of the Oachira Vrischikam festival. Millions of devotees from all corners of India had made their way to the temple. However, in that moment, Renjini was struggling to muster any belief in the divine. As she put down the phone receiver, she instinctively called her husband to check on the well-being of their children.

A few minutes later, Jijimol was at Mahilamandiram. The superintendent of the shelter home was waiting at the gate to welcome the officer. Jijimol promptly refused an offer for tea and requested to be taken to Pooja's room immediately. All Jijimol saw on her walk from the entry of the rescue centre to the room were desolate eyes of women and children narrating stories of unfathomable evil. The superintendent told her about a few of the women who had been abandoned by their families for fear of social ostracism. The sight of these women made Jijimol count her many blessings in life.

As Jijimol entered the room, Pooja was sitting on the ground and staring out of the lone window. Geetha was sitting next to her, lost in thought. Jijimol cleared her throat and Geetha got up on seeing a person in uniform. Pooja was still motionless. Jijimol signalled Geetha to sit and took a seat on the only chair in the room. Jijimol experienced an ominous weight in the atmosphere. She had been in rooms with hardened criminals and never felt that kind of emptiness but in this space with a juvenile victim, she felt a rush of emotions.

Clearing her throat again, Jijimol addressed Pooja, 'We will be taking you to a doctor later in the evening. There is nothing to worry about.'

While Geetha registered some relief on her face, Pooja continued to be expressionless. She could not banish the thought of the impact her ordeal was bound to have on her family. She was choking on her own guilt.

Over the next few hours, Jijimol recorded Pooja's official statement. Pooja spoke in a robot-like voice but managed to recount her tribulations in great depth. While the statement was being recorded, Renjini had arrived in a police jeep to take Pooja to the Government Victoria Hospital. Renjini also collected the statement recorded by Jijimol to be sent to her colleague at the Oachira police station.

Based on Pooja's statement, an FIR was lodged at the Oachira police station by Constable Vinod Chandran. The Sections included were 376 Indian Penal Code (IPC) which deals with punishment for rape, Section 3 read with Section 4 of the Protection of Children from Sexual Offences (POCSO) Act[3] and Section 23 of the Juvenile Justice Act[4]. A request for Pooja's medical report and the recording of her statement by a judicial magistrate was also issued.

---

[3]Section 3 and Section 4 of the POCSO Act deal with penetrative sexual assault and the punishment for it.

[4]Section 23 of the Juvenile Justice (Care and Protection of Children) Act, 2000, deals with punishment for cruelty to juveniles or children.

Easier Than Living

Dr Beena was the gynaecologist on duty at the Government Victoria Hospital when Pooja was rolled in on a wheelchair by Renjini. It was not that Pooja couldn't walk, she had just lost the will to. Geetha was sombrely walking to the left of the wheelchair. Dr Beena had been briefed about the case on a phone call by a sub-inspector. She was fully aware of the sensitivity of the matter and the fragile state of the victim.

'I will examine her in the private ward. Please do not worry.' Dr Beena reassured Geetha and Renjini, both of whom wore matter-of-fact expressions.

Dr Beena quickly read through the statement Pooja had given Jijimol and noted whatever was relevant to the medical examination in a pocket-sized diary. Then she requested Geetha and Renjini to wait outside while she examined Pooja in the private ward.

In the ward, Dr Beena asked Pooja about the history of bleeding after she had jammed the bottle into her belly. Pooja told the doctor that the bleeding had been copious initially but died down later.

'This might hurt a bit,' Dr Beena said as she checked for signs of sexual assault. Pooja was emotionless. Dr Beena found that the hymen was completely torn at the 2 o'clock and the 7 o'clock position. This finding was consistent with Pooja's statement—Satheesh had been both forceful and violent. While she had conducted many of these tests, every time Dr Beena came across a rape victim, her heart sank. The degree of damage in Pooja's case made even the doctor grimace.

'Pooja, how are you feeling?' Dr Beena asked her just after the test.

'I feel nothing, doctor.'

'Does it still hurt?'

'Everything hurts but nothing does.'

'I cannot say that I understand your pain, Pooja, but you must tell me about the pain in your vagina so that I can help you.'

'It feels numb. I feel punished by God. I will never feel pleasure.'

'That is not true, Pooja. I will prescribe some medicines and you will feel better. About the rest, I will talk to your mother.'

Dr Beena then conducted a pregnancy test which was a weak positive. To corroborate her findings, she recommended an ultrasound and a Beta HCG test. The ultrasound confirmed that Pooja was indeed with child and the blow with the bottle had proved fatal to the baby. She needed surgery.

Pooja's reports were an official confirmation of the

horrors she had lived through. Dr Beena handed them over to Renjini and gave a list of medicines to Geetha. She also asked Geetha to get a psychological evaluation of Pooja done at the earliest.

∞

The following day, 7th January, Pooja was taken by Renjini to the office of the Chief Judicial Magistrate who recorded her statement under Section 164 of the Criminal Procedure Code.[5]

Kerala Police also swung into action under ACP Anil Kumar. Scene *mahazar*s (crime scene maps) were prepared for both Pooja-Shraddha and Sooryabhavanam. The garments Pooja had worn at the time of the assault were also seized and added to the body of evidence.

While a lot of groundwork had been done by February itself, the obvious roadblock for the investigating authorities of Kerala Police was that Satheesh had, meanwhile, fled to Riyadh in the Kingdom of Saudi Arabia where he was employed as a tile worker. No rape accused had ever been extradited to India from any country, and the knowledge of Satheesh's flight from India dampened the enthusiasm of the police.

Time passed quickly for the investigators as they tried to collect all available evidence to present a fool-proof plea of extradition to the Saudi authorities. A lookout

---

[5]Recording of confessions and statements by competent Metropolitan Magistrate or Judicial Magistrate.

notice[6] was issued by the police in case Satheesh tried to undertake any international travel. In addition, a red corner notice[7] (RCN) was broadcast for Satheesh's extradition. However, the promptness of Kerala Police was not replicated in Saudi and the increased workload meant that Pooja's file started to gather dust.

By May, Pooja had begun to lose hope of any justice. She had been made aware by Renjini of the long road that extradition often is and also knew that with the passage of time, other cases crying for attention would eventually take precedence. She kept to herself in Mahilamandiram and never shared the extreme churn she felt in the pit of her stomach on a daily basis.

Geetha and Vinaykumar made every effort to keep their daughter in good spirits. They would bring her old pictures of her childhood and also video messages from her sisters. Geetha would also cook some of Pooja's favourite dishes. Gopikumar, too, visited Pooja but could not look her in the eye. He was reeling under the guilt of having brought Satheesh in contact with the family. While Pooja was always cordial to the visitors, she never showed real happiness. Her mind was always inundated with flashes of the menace on Satheesh's face.

---

[6]It is also known as the lookout circular (LOC). It is used for nabbing wanted people or criminals at international borders, international airports, maritime areas, ports, etc.

[7]A red corner notice is a request to law enforcement worldwide to locate and provisionally arrest a person pending extradition, surrender, or similar legal action.

It was after months of little conversation that Pooja finally spoke to her father in June.

'Achan… Am I dirty?'

'No, Pooja. You are a piece of our hearts, so beautiful and so pure.'

'But he has imprinted himself on me. The stains will never go.'

'Don't say that. You have done nothing wrong. What happened is my mistake, not yours. I placed my trust in the devil.'

'Achan, what will my future be? With this blot, no one will ever look at me without pity. Not even you.'

'We are proud of you. And you will find a way.'

'Yes, I will have to find a way.'

'Remember how we used to walk through the paddy fields when you were a kid, and you always led the way? That is who you are—a leader. Never forget that.'

Pooja's mind went back to a vivid memory—her running through the paddy fields and hiding behind trees where her family would not be able to find her.

'Achan, remember how much you used to worry every time I hid behind the trees? Your frustration often came out on Upasana and Shraddha.'

'How can I forget? You were so naughty, so fiercely independent.'

'I want to be like that again, Achan. I really want to.'

'That will happen soon, Pooja. Then we will go home.'

'I will go home only after Uncle Satheesh is behind bars.'

'Yes, Pooja. They will catch him soon.'

'Will they?'

'He has his wife and children here. For how long can he stay in Saudi?'

'Then we will go home.' Pooja feigned a smile.

Vinaykumar kissed his daughter on the forehead as the visiting hours came to a close. As he turned around to get a glimpse of her before leaving, he saw a genuine smile on her face for the first time in months. He thought that there was perhaps a glimmer of hope after all. That night, after months, he got some sleep.

The next morning, Pooja was found hanging in her room by an attendant at Mahilamandiram.

A Double Blow

The news of Pooja's demise took away whatever little life was left in Pooja-Shraddha. There was stunned silence in a home which was still full of people. All that could be heard were persistent silent sobs and occasional wails. There was half an expectation that Pooja would suddenly show up with a school bag on her shoulders, a couple of paddy leaves in hand.

Geetha was trying to hold her family together by showing them a rosy picture of possible justice for Pooja. She realized that in the circumstances that prevailed, everyone around, particularly Vinaykumar, needed a reason to continue living. The deaths all of them had died within, could not become a reason to sacrifice the future of the two other daughters in the family.

'Pooja is in a better place,' Geetha would sometimes declare.

At other times, she would say, 'She was too innocent for this world.'

The others would listen in silence and sometimes briefly nod in acknowledgement.

Gopikumar, on the other hand, had no one to talk to. Upon receiving the news of Pooja's passing, he remained mum for a while and then made his way to a bridge on the sea. With each rising wave, a tsunami of guilt grew in his heart. He felt personally responsible for Pooja's fate because Satheesh was originally his friend.

Beads of sweat assembled on Gopikumar's forehead even on that pleasant winter afternoon. His heart pounded through his slightly built frame and each of his ribs felt like an instrument of torture. He stared vacantly at the sky.

'Why? Aaaaaaaa…' He shouted in anguish.

'Aaaaaaaa…' His cries were heard only by the crows that sat on one end of the bridge.

After about fifteen minutes of shouting relentlessly, Gopikumar was exhausted. He sat on the metal railing of the bridge to get some rest. A crow flew in out of nowhere and its sudden appearance made Gopikumar fall onto the road behind him. As he got up, he felt the crow, which was now sitting on the railing, looking him in the eye. A wave grew behind the bird making it look larger and fearsome. The splash of the water from the wave reached Gopikumar and the pool of water that formed next to him appeared crimson to his eyes. He felt a sense of doom and hurriedly made his way home.

Later that night, Gopikumar was checking the firmness of the rope he had tied to the ceiling fan in his bedroom. The bed had been shifted to one side of the room and replaced by a chair on which Gopikumar stood. On the bed was a Malayali newspaper with the headline:

'Truth behind how Vijay Mallya fled India.' It was eerily quiet, save for the buzz of crickets in the neighbourhood. As Gopikumar put the noose around his neck, nothing but guilt continued to fill his being. He uttered, 'I am sorry, Pooja,' to an empty room before closing his eyes and kicking the chair away.

Merin

King Khalid International Airport, Riyadh, 16 July 2019

Just behind Merin Joseph, the slightly built Thakshak Satheesh was the last to board the flight. Flanked by ACP Anil Kumar and Inspector Prakash, he was in a Saudi prisoner's uniform. The uniform was adequately prisoner-like, certainly blue enough to identify him in a crowd of immaculately attired airline passengers. He immediately drew the attention of those already in the aircraft. Hushed murmurs made their way down the aisle as Satheesh was seated in the front row between the officers detaining him. Merin was seated across the aisle in the same row.

The cops made it a point to avoid any interaction with the passengers. Quelling the curiosity of their fellow travellers was low on the list of extradition requirements. They needed to keep the operation low-key to the extent possible. They were on the cusp of pulling off something unprecedented—the first extradition, that too of a first rape accused, from Saudi Arabia to India. They had managed to overcome several barriers, not the least of which was to meet the daunting two-week deadline to get custody of Satheesh.

The aircraft was wheels up soon. A sense of achievement began to overwhelm the team as the plane levelled off at cruising altitude. As the cabin went dark, Merin's emotions began to take off. A flashback of the previous days where the team had been able to navigate through unforeseen hurdles made her heart swell with emotions. She allowed herself a few silent tears. She knew in that moment that she truly belonged in the khaki.

Union Public Service Commission, New Delhi, 3 May 2013

The haloed precincts of the Union Public Service Commission (UPSC) in New Delhi were abuzz with anticipation. The final results of the coveted All-India Services examination were to be announced. Scores of faces, some bright and young, others weathered by previous disappointments, awaited the results outside the gate of the main building.

Twenty-three-year-old Merin Joseph stood among this teeming crowd. Merin had a track record of academic excellence. She had done her schooling from the Convent of Jesus and Mary in Delhi where she had topped her batch. Her excellent marks in the intermediate examination had enabled her to secure a place in the prestigious St. Stephen's College for a Bachelor's in History. She went on to do both her graduation and post-graduation from that institution, and continued to top the merit list.

Merin had always been academically inclined. Her mother, Merina George, had inculcated in Merin a deep-seated love for the written word. Her early exposure to books and libraries had made her an avid reader. While she enjoyed the occasional outdoor sport, Merin's time was best spent in long corridors stacked with volumes. She did run a few races during her days in school but her focus was almost squarely on the scholarly part of the education spectrum.

In her college days in Delhi, like other students, she too enjoyed hanging around in the college campus, yet her focus on studies was so strong that 'idling around' was something she detested. While others were lost in conversations and games over umpteen cups of tea and coffee in the canteen, she would be lost in tomes which exercised an irresistible pull on her. Her circle of friends was small. The choice of friends was so made that her focus on books remained intact. Thus she was a person whose world was shared by a few, and reading was what she thought was the best way to live a meaningful life. Her exposure to fellow students was restricted owing to her reticence and she found the college atmosphere a bit intimidating.

Merin came from a family with a tradition of public

service. Her father was a public servant. He had joined the Indian Economic Service in 1979. Her mother was a school teacher. The reason Merin had spent most of her life in Delhi was her father's posting in the national capital. He was also a source of constant encouragement for Merin through all her ups and downs in life. His support for her ambitions was the kind most daughters yearn for. He had backed her to the hilt when she had made the decision to appear for the UPSC examination. Merin's mother made sure that all the basics were taken care of while she was preparing for the civil services examination during her post-graduation. Both parents were keen to see their daughter fulfil her dream of becoming a public servant.

∞

Merin's Home, New Delhi, 2001

'Joseph, Merin is clearly cut out to follow an academic career. I can see in her a hunger to gather knowledge. At her age, few youngsters spend so much time in the library as she does,' a somewhat concerned mother confided in her husband.

Dr Joseph Abraham thought for a while and spoke reassuringly, 'Yes, I see that she pores over whatever books she can lay her hands on. Still, I am glad that she isn't a complete bookworm as is clear from her performance as an athlete. She has won a few races at school, and when

I look at her, I find that if she embarks upon a career which requires her to be active in outdoor work, she will not be found wanting.'

Merina George responded, 'Indeed, there is no doubt that she is excelling as a student. Her complete concentration on books gives me the feeling that she might choose a career like mine. She will make a fine teacher.'

'Of course, she has all the makings of an educator. Yet, isn't it a bit too early to bother about her career? All I can see is that we have a disciplined daughter whose focus is on academic excellence. She will surely land a career of which we will be proud,' was the doting father's response.

This conversation took place in 2001 while Merin was a student of the Convent of Jesus and Mary in New Delhi. It was in the spring of the same year when Merin was driving to India Gate with the parents and her brother to enjoy an evening in the lawns there. As the car passed in front of the premises of UPSC on Shahjahan Road, Joseph pointed towards the pink-and-grey building to tell his children that the competitive examination which led to his selection to the Economic Service was conducted by UPSC. He went on to tell them that the Commission is the body which conducts the most significant examinations for the selection of the country's brightest students to the top echelons of government.

At the India Gate lawns, the conversation between the curious Merin and the indulgent father continued to be about UPSC.

'Merin, the most estimable competition that the Commission conducts is one through which the country's top civil servants are selected. The Civil Services Examination is one dream that millions of Indians share. They aspire to services such as the Indian Foreign Service (IFS), the Indian Administrative Service (IAS) and the Indian Police Service (IPS). These are by far the most sought-after government jobs for youngsters who are unwilling to settle for the second best. Even engineers and doctors compete!'

'Papa, are women officers comfortable in a cop's job? Is the IPS a preferred choice for women aspirants to the civil services?'

'Yes, Merin. The trend set by Kiran Bedi, the first woman to enter the IPS, has really caught on. Following her, there have been dozens of women who have joined this challenging service. One can say that they are as good as any other officer. However, no one has gathered the kind of fandom that Kiran Bedi enjoys. Many young women look up to her as a role model.'

'Papa, tell me more. I am very interested to work for the selection to the civil services,' the young Merin said.

'Including the IPS?'

'Yes, of course, Papa!' Merin smiled.

Merin was driven by ambition. Her dreams stretched far beyond the walls that society traditionally builds for women. She was never one to depend on luck and was willing to toil in trying circumstances to achieve her dreams. She believed in the Dutch artist Vincent Van Gogh's words, 'I dream of painting and then I paint my dream.'

After the drive with her father on Shahjahan Road, and learning about the civil services, she concentrated her efforts on breaking into a walk of life where even now only a few women venture. It is a heavily male-dominated domain, and despite the good name that many of her woman predecessors and colleagues had earned through their grit, determination, hard work, never-say-die spirit and skill, men were still holding on to the services as their sole preserve in which women were to be seen as the exception to the rule.

Interestingly, before taking the UPSC plunge, the other dreams that Merin had were far removed from the rough and tumble of police life. She imagined herself to be a researcher. Her deep interest in history made her believe that she would make a name for herself in the world of historians. She also saw herself in the avatar of a professor enlightening generations of knowledge-seekers. Merin had also toyed with the idea of becoming a writer. She had an interest in the culinary arts and briefly even entertained the thought of becoming a professional chef. Next on her bucket list was being an interior designer, a career which she found exciting. These interests did not translate into her eventual career but gave her the innate ability to respect and empathize with professionals from myriad walks of life.

It was the call of the khaki that made Merin feel most focused. She had assessed that her larger objective in life, that of bringing succour to the oppressed and the violated, would be best served in her assignments as a top cop. It was a job, she imagined, that would challenge her all the time to achieve more, do better. The childhood characteristic of being a learner gave her the confidence that in the different assignments she lands, there would be the opportunity to enhance the base of her professional knowledge and she would be able to upgrade her skills, thereby becoming increasingly more competent as the years would pass.

Union Public Service Commission, New Delhi, 3 May 2013

The results are usually declared in a cut-and-dried manner. The romanticization of a favourable outcome is what follows in the mind of a successful examinee. When the stakes are as high as getting into an All-India Service, not just those who make it to the coveted jobs but their entire locality celebrates. With social media catching on, prominent politicians also tweet about the success stories from their constituencies. The unbridled joy of a few drowns out the far greater number of wails of those who do not make the cut.

Merin had been an ace student through all of her

academic life but this was her first attempt at the All-India Services examination. This entrance examination is often seen as the battlefield where all competitors have an equal chance and the 'toppers' from schools and colleges do not have any leverage. Success in the maiden attempt, particularly after the trend of coaching institutions where students prepare for years, has become increasingly rare. Many give the exam a shot just to understand the format and develop a keener understanding of how far the target is.

And just like that, the results were out!

Dr Joseph Abraham and Merina George had reason to celebrate. Merin had hit the bull's eye. She had achieved the 188th rank in the examination. The rank was high enough to get her the second choice—IPS.

Merin had not set her eyes on just one service. She had, like most others, given IAS as her first preference followed by IPS. At twenty-two, when she appeared for the competition, her knowledge of the nuances and factors associated with the different services on offer was hazy at best. Yet when she found herself in the IPS list, she could not help fantasizing herself wearing a resplendent khaki uniform—shining metal on the shoulders, medals in their dazzling glory on the chest, the peak cap with the national symbol sitting prominently like a jewel in a crown. She visualized striding into dens of criminals, taking them head-on, and demolishing their gangs one after another. The thought of following in the footsteps of Kiran Bedi, whose zeal for service had become embedded in her ever since the conversation with her father at the India Gate lawns, filled her with unparalleled enthusiasm. Now that the name 'Merin Joseph' was on the list, she had taken a step closer to living her dream.

Finding Her Feet

Merin's Home, New Delhi

The frenzied activity of packing for travel is never without its last-minute hiccups. Merin, a stickler for detail in all she did, had the confidence that the checklist she had prepared covered all her requirements from head to toe. Yet, she was not without a certain degree of nervousness about the new life that awaited her. From the hot and sultry national capital to the beautiful town which people called the queen of hills—Mussoorie, the distance was not a challenge, yet a traveller had many miles to travel to embrace an altogether new life. The transformation from a student to a person holding a position which called for great measures of maturity and responsibility was an undercurrent which had the youngster on tenterhooks.

'Merin, have you kept enough warm clothing for the hill station. It's time for the monsoon to arrive, and the temperatures would dive low,' Merina, her mom, reminded her for the fourth time in an hour.

'Yes, Mom. You have told me earlier as well. Don't worry, I have taken all care,' Merin replied, keeping her cool.

'Yes, Merin. I was only making sure. We do not have such cold weather in Kerala.'

'Mom, thank you. But this was the fourth time,' Merin laughed.

Just then Merin's Dad, Joseph came in. He asked, 'Merin, make sure that you have the appointment letter with you. And don't forget to carry photo IDs.'

'Yes Dad, these papers made their way in earliest. The appointment letter is a treasure. It gives me goosebumps when I think that this letter begins with the words "The President of India is pleased to appoint…" I know you also must have treasured a similarly worded letter when it came your way decades earlier.'

'Yes, I still have the letter with me. Now, *priya makal* (beloved daughter), you have made me and your mom proud.'

The family came together in a warm embrace. No words were exchanged, yet emotions ran high—all three had tears in their eyes.

Just then Merin's brother, Abraham, came in and joined the hug, complaining, 'Why leave me out?'

❧

Merin often wondered if all the great ideas of social justice were within the ambit of the work she had ahead of her as a cop. Early in her training as a civil servant, she exchanged thoughts with her batchmates at the foundation course[8] in the Lal Bahadur Shastri National Academy of Administration (LBSNAA), Mussoorie.

One of her best buddies at the Academy was Vinayak Varma. The two hit it off due to their deep and common interest in books, and it was no wonder that the world of the written word became their beat. Being in the library was the time they both looked forward to. Later, in the mess lounge, they would have long chats about almost everything under and even beyond the sun. Vinayak was a lawyer prior to joining the Academy and had worked for a corporate law firm in London. He was incredibly well-read and never ran short of information and ideas in endless engaging conversations.

The year they were in the Academy at Mussoorie, India was witnessing a huge political upheaval. The government at the Centre had faced heat on multiple fronts. A large number of alleged scandals were brought into focus by the movement led by Anna Hazare in 2011. The gruesome Nirbhaya rape and murder in December 2012 which had shaken the nation, impacted the citizens as few cases had done. There were prolonged demonstrations in the streets of New Delhi and many other cities which ultimately led to the formation of a committee under a retired Supreme Court judge to examine ways to make the rape

[8]The initial training schedule common for probationers of all services selected through the UPSC examination, this is held at the LBSNAA, Mussoorie, and at a couple of other centres.

law more stringent and provide better security to women in public places. Naturally, this was the burning topic of the day when the batch of officer trainees converged at the Academy in 2013. Vinayak, a lawyer by education, and Merin, a cop in the making, had a lot to discuss.

'Merin, I am disappointed that the police were lax in their response when the early information of the incident reached them. This lays bare the inadequacy of the law-and-order machinery even in the heart of the national capital,' lamented Vinayak.

'Of course, having been a Delhiite myself, I know dangers lurk for women in all nooks and corners. Every time I returned home after college or other places, I said a silent "Thank you, God" for having protected me. But I will not blame the police alone for the rot. There are a lot of other players who contribute,' Merin responded.

'So, you are already defending the cops! Merin, you are learning fast, I must say,' Vinayak chuckled.

'Come on, Vin. Is it not a fact that we need to have a look at the quantum of punishment, the speed of trials and the need for witness protection?'

'Yes, of course, I agree that we cannot overlook the other loopholes. Yet, the first responders need to be a picture of efficiency and alacrity. Wasn't that missing, Merin?'

'I am keen to make a dent in that. We have to make our colleagues at all levels a lot more sensitive to the pains of those who are victims of crime. I hope to be in a position one day to make that happen.'

After a brief period of reflection, Vinayak said, 'Merin, there are people from all segments of our society who have been waiting for the wrongs they have endured to be redressed. I am sure sensitive cops can make some difference, and you are going to be one of them.'

'Yes, Vin. There must be many cases lying dormant. Criminals must be roaming about with impunity, looking for opportunities to strike again. This has been brought out in an article I read in a magazine this morning. What is worse is that cases which are languishing due to the indifference of the investigating officers are mostly ones where the victims come from underprivileged sections of our society. Women, children, helpless poor people…they are all waiting for relief.'

'I'm so glad you have a roadmap etched in your thoughts. I hope you will get the opportunities to make a mark.'

'I'm driven a lot by the sheer opportunity and scope of the positions we occupy and the huge expectations that people have from us. The plight of the underprivileged and of those without access to power genuinely touches a chord with me. It's tough to not strive to rise up to those expectations constantly!' Merin responded.

'Come on, Merin! That sounds like a speech from a seasoned politician,' Vinayak said light-heartedly.

'The difference is, I mean every word of what I'm saying, unlike the netas.' Both the youngsters laughed.

∞

Mussoorie was so completely removed from the hustle of

New Delhi—quiet, pleasant and enchanting. There were new friends to be made, many of them people with huge inventories of knowledge and mind-boggling life stories, new things to learn and, above all, the first introduction to a feeling of freedom. Decisions, small and big, were to be made without the guidance of parents. While this was a little difficult to begin with, the idea of being on one's own was exciting. Merin was not even aware that slowly she was gaining the maturity to be independent, to be a decision-maker.

The days of the first phase of the training were full of wonder, excitement and learning. Friday evenings in the Academy lounge were a great pleasure, a welcome for the much looked-forward-to weekend. Conversations, which seldom led to bickering among the group of newly-made friends, and at times based on little substance, were nevertheless of immense value to make her understand people better, know the art of sifting the chaff from the grain, and to generally develop an acute sense of judgement of true value.

The long walks from Charleville to Picture Palace were never without the excitement that only seemed possible in hill stations. Families from the plains, some from nearby towns of Uttar Pradesh, and others from Delhi, Punjab and Haryana, presented a picture of the variety that India had. It was interesting to notice that these groups almost always looked true to the stereotypes they were associated with in their manners, street behaviour, enjoyment of food at restaurants and roadside eateries, etc. The few from the southern states of India who covered the long distance to be in the cool climes stood apart in their ideas of how to spend a few days holidaying.

For the officer trainee group, chaat in Kulri Bazar, softie at Chic Chocolate, the jalebi at Laxmi, were all major draws. One of their favourite halts was the Band Stand near the Library. That is where a lot of tourists would also converge and be the subjects of some interesting observations by the young recruits.

'Look at that guy with those gaudy clothes. I am sure he is from Delhi,' said Sudhakar, a Tamilian who always had a sarcastic take on the Delhiwallas, adding for good effect, 'must have made money through dirty means.'

'Why? Do you think it's only Delhiwallas who make money on the sly?' asked Merin.

'Not always, but often. The capital stinks of its capital frauds.'

'Come on, let's accept it, Delhi is not alone in this.'

'Look at that brat making such a scene, shouting at the top of his voice and demanding toys from his parents. What a spoilt child. And his parents are lost in their own world, not bothering to take notice of their child's clamorous entreaties,' was Sudha's observation.

'Sudha, with this kind of concern for seeing well-behaved kids, you are sure to land in the Ministry of Women and Child Development one day,' quipped Merin.

That many who came to holiday in the serene surroundings of the lovely hill town often had very antithetical ideas about the best way to spend their precious time, away from the worries of the cities they came from, amused the officer trainees. A frequently witnessed scene was the arrival of a family in a taxi, with the portly man slipping out of the seat with some effort and a grunt, followed by an equally rotund wife and fast-food-eating, well-filled-out kids. The man would be surrounded by hotel touts attracting his attention, sooner than he would've alighted from the taxi, with offers of service which ranged from a colour TV in the room to an AC for spending time comfortably.

'Imagine coming to Mussoorie and then having the AC carrot dangled in front of you, and even falling for it,' Merin would often exclaim, and add, 'topped with the enticement to spend time in the closed room!'

'That the idea of being in an idyllic tourist town in the Himalayas is to enjoy the cool breeze and the natural beauty of the hills seems to be far from their imagination,' Vinayak would say.

'The wife, meanwhile, must have decided where she would do her shopping for trinkets, which, she would know very well, are also available in her own city, and at much lower prices too. But such is the mood that shopping becomes a key ritual to go through, ultimately picking up stuff which figured on no shopping list... Haha...' Merin laughed.

'Look at us writing a whole movie script! Are we getting into the wrong profession?' Sudhakar joked.

All the probationers broke into a hearty laugh.

~

Sardar Vallabhbhai Patel National Police Academy (SVPNPA), Hyderabad

'*Aapse nahin hoga! Arre, kaii aadmi bhi rassi pe nahin chadh paate. Chhodo. Kuchh muscle banaao...phir try karna.*' (You will not be able to do it! Even some men fail to climb to the top of the rope. Leave it. First grow some muscle, and then try it.) The Ustad spat out those words so dismissively that Merin was almost on the verge of tears.

The other officer trainees tried to hide their reactions—mostly mocking her. There was, of course, Vinayak, who seemed to be genuinely sympathetic to Merin. He did not hold back, 'Ustad, this is not right. You are ridiculing an officer. She is a woman, and equally capable, if not better, than many men in the squad. You should stick to training us without showing your offensive prejudice.'

The Ustad did not expect such a response, 'How dare you say this to an Ustad? You know I can punish you here, and even report to the ADOD (Assistant Director, Outdoor Training). He will see to it that you learn your lesson once and for all.'

'Ustad, I request you to not insult an OT (officer trainee) like you did Merin. This is not proper. You should teach, not make fun or make sexist remarks.'

'So you will teach me how I should train? *Aap jaise darjanon ko sikha chuka hoon.*' (I have taught dozens like you.)

'Ustad, let us accept it that it is not merely Merin who finds climbing the rope a tough ask. There is also Raj, Nayak and Mohan who are not up to this task. Why do you single out Merin? Is it because she is a girl?'

The Ustad looked flustered, but immediately found an escape. 'I know climbing the rope is not everybody's cup of tea. Not just officer Merin. I mean to help her so that she becomes stronger.' After a brief pause, he shouted, 'Okay, let's get on with the exercises. We just have a few minutes left in this session.'

Later, in her room, Vinayak was consoling her, 'Merin, you are one of the best in the batch. I know at least a dozen other trainees who find climbing the rope difficult. Haven't you seen how Raj, Nayak and Mohan just hold the rope and suspend themselves at the beginning of the climb? But they are not treated like you were. This bias is unacceptable. We must take it up with the ADOD.'

'Certainly not, Vinayak,' Merin shot back with such vehemence that her friend was shocked. She continued, 'I can't deny that I am not comfortable with some of the taxing physical demands of outdoor training. The vigorous session of PT in the morning, followed by the drill with that monster 5-kg rifle, and then a rushed shower and quick breakfast; all this is too much of work with no time for a breather. Minutes later, we are in the indoor classes. It's hard to keep awake...especially in those boring law classes. It's all due to the routine on the parade ground, and, to be honest, I must admit that the physical strain really drains me of all my energy.

'Vinayak, please don't conclude that I want to run away from all the strain. Do you remember my swimming test and how I had to dive into the deep end of the pool? It made me muster up all the courage I had and it was a moment I will never forget. After the test, I did the deep end dive from the ten-feet diving board twice more, just to boost my confidence. So, it's not as if I am shirking or shamming.'

After a pause, she said, 'You know what I find most irritating? It's that exercise of first pulling apart all the parts of a weapon, and then reassembling it, only to repeat this many times over. Tell me, Vinayak, what is the advantage of all this? At the end of it, I am left with bruised fingers which ache for hours. My fingers are, after all, so much more delicate than yours or most others'.'

'Look at the positive side of the weapon training, Merin. Isn't firing and target practice exciting?'

'Yes, Vinayak. I also enjoy firing. It is adrenaline inducing. I get a high as it gives me the feeling of power; it makes me believe that I can deal with the toughest challenges. No criminal will be able to stand up to me. I am talking about disassembling and then putting together the weapon; I am not convinced that this needs to be done every day. It leaves me physically exhausted.'

'It is not just you who has a problem with physical fatigue, isn't it true that many of our batchmates, me included, are fagged out most of the day?' Vinayak added, 'My objection to Ustad was about his unacceptable sexist jibe. I think this must stop. Now women are there in a fairly large number in the service. I see no scope for such prejudice. You must raise your voice about this.'

'I agree that the trainers should be sensitive and not have gender prejudices, but I would avoid being singled out for raising my voice against the Ustad.' After a pause, she added, 'And we have Soman Sir, our DI (drill instructor), the kindest man you will ever come across. We can share our problem with him any time. Let us not take it to any level above him. He will be the right person to guide us. I am sure he will help *makra*s (slackers) like me when I am caught in this situation.'

Both Merin and Vinayak had a laugh. Makra was DI Soman's favourite term of endearment when he addressed the officer trainees.

'Oh yes, Soman Sir is not only kind and understanding, he is also a much-respected instructor, the senior-most among all the DIs. Hasn't he cast a web of affection around all of us trainees? He is considerate yet firm.'

'And we are lucky to have such good friends in the batch. Our best buddies like Jaidev, our squad mates Suman, Karthik, Rituraj, Chanchal, Jaggu, are all there. So, we have a great cushion to absorb all the discomfort that may come our way. Jaidev is also going to be with you in the Kerala cadre. When all these friends are there, you don't have to worry.'

Merin nodded her head in agreement, and said, 'My squad mates are all so incredibly nice. I am lucky to be in such a laid-back, friendly squad. I am always completely at ease with each one of them. Of course, the squad mates are a mix of enthusiasm, cheer and good humour. You have seen how I invariably crack up with laughter at their wisecracks and harmless jokes. Thank you, Vinayak. You have really helped me.'

Vinayak couldn't suppress a tired yawn, and said, 'Okay, Merin. I have a tutorial to write, so I am going to my room. You look tired. Take a nap.'

'Oh, Vinayak! You said it... I must immediately lie down and doze off. I am too tired and I don't want to sleep through the indoor lectures again. At this rate, passing the tough written tests will call for much preparation. Good night, friend. You are a great source of strength.'

Next morning as she opened her eyes, it was a Sunday and Merin thought of skipping breakfast. No sooner had she thought of stretching her sleep longer did she remember that one of the items on the Sunday breakfast menu was on her list of favourites—*poha* (flattened rice-based snack). She loved this savoury, and was in no mood to miss it. As she quickly tidied herself up to go to the mess, she had a smile on her face. She started to think about some of the delicacies which were served in the mess—the weekend biryani, chicken *do pyaza* (literally 'two onions'; dish prepared with two different types of onions), and, of course, the mouth-watering desserts. The thought of the IPS mess food helped her overcome the previous evening's misery on account of the Ustad's remarks. She trotted to the dining hall with a smile on her face.

'Am I really up to it?'

'Am I deluding myself?'

'Wasn't I stupid in choosing something for which I am a total misfit?'

A tired, completely exhausted Merin was asking these questions of herself, sitting on a culvert and leaning on a rifle she was carrying. She was at kilometre thirty in a route march of forty-two kilometres.

She was looking at the limited supply of water she was allowed to carry. She knew that a sip or two of the Earth's greatest offering would do her good, but she was rationing the little quantity she had in the bottle.

In a strange way she was reminded that the human body has close to six hundred muscles and a hundred and eighty-five joints—for all of them were paining excruciatingly. A quick estimate gave her the feeling that she had pain in some she had never before known existed. All muscles and joints were protesting…asking for immediate relief. A bed, of any description, was what her body craved for.

She couldn't hold back her tears as she asked herself, 'Is the IPS going to be a lifelong nightmare like this?'

The village visits and treks on the rugged stretches in the hills around Mussoorie during the foundation course, with friends in their element, fun and frolic all around, were so pleasant compared to what she was experiencing now…a forty-two-kilometre taxing march, the heavy rifle, the need to reach the destination within a stipulated time, no food to eat, not even enough water to quench her thirst, and no exchange of pleasant conversations with friends. Just hell, with no sight of even a remote sign of relief was all that was in store for her.

Did she err in her judgement? Was she up to the rigours of a tough job?

The announcement that an essay competition was being organized for the officers under training at the NPA was received with a mixed response. While many felt that it was an imposition on an already formidable burden, some took it in their stride—much like a fait accompli. A few looked forward to competing with their peers and proving their superiority. Then there were those truly enthusiastic ones who thought that the opportunity success in the competition offered was priceless. Merin belonged to the last group.

The winner of the competition would get the opportunity to represent India in the Youth20 (Y20)[9]

---

[9]Youth Summit which links into the wider G20 leaders' summit to be held later in 2014 in Australia. The Y20 Summit is the official platform for young people from across G20 countries to engage in policy discussions on the most pressing global economic challenges and generate innovative solutions which will be presented to the G20 Leaders' Summit for consideration in their discussions.

What is G20? The Group of Twenty (G20) is a forum for international economic cooperation and decision-making. It is made up of 19 countries plus the European Union. It meets regularly to discuss ways to strengthen the global economy, discuss economic reform and improve financial regulation. *Ref:* y20-faq.pdf (myd.govt.nz).

Summit in Sydney. This was indeed a strong incentive, especially for the young IPS officers, many of whom had never set foot on foreign soil.

Heartbeats were racing on result day, and Merin was among the officer trainees in a state of suspense. She knew that the evaluation of the essays was being done by the Staff College and this gave her the assurance that only merit would determine who touched the finishing tape first. And then the news came—Merin was the one!

The selection, based purely on her writing acumen and knowledge, renewed her faith in her decision to opt for the rigours of the service she had chosen for herself; many doubts which had assailed her at one time were significantly diluted. Merin was the youngest participant in the Y20 Youth Summit. Her glee on being selected was multiplied by the fact that it presented her with the prospect of her first visit to a foreign country.

The participants spent five days in Sydney. It was an enriching experience for Merin. Seeing a foreign city, attending a large-scale international conference with global participation, networking, and the sheer excitement of the sights and sounds of a city like Sydney added new dimensions to her world view. Witnessing from the iconic Opera House the bustling Circular Quay on one end, while savouring the peace of the yachts and ferries passing under the Harbour Bridge on the other, made Merin feel infinite for a few moments. Her confidence both as a person and a cop grew significantly through these experiences.

The event lasted only five days, yet the impact was long-lasting. Merin brushed shoulders with peers from across the globe and gathered from them the varying concerns and plans different ethnicities had for the future. This broadened her own horizon and a lot more filled her thoughts than what had been her repertoire till then.

The topics that were discussed at the Summit made her feel like a global citizen. Subjects such as labour and mobility, growth and jobs, and climate change were the focus at the Summit. The young participants were assigned to different teams and they were asked to come up with recommendations for strategizing responses to various problems.

A major takeaway for Merin was the learning that the world is bigger than it appears to us and we are far less important than what we think. She also understood that global decision-making is participative in many ways though countries can exert influence based on their relative strengths. This was her first brush with the finer nuances of international diplomacy.

This visit to Sydney made Merin a person who was a lot more self-assured, one who was ready to be a leader.

While Merin was still an officer under training at the NPA, a photo of hers in uniform went viral on social media identifying her falsely as Kochi's 'hot' new Assistant Commissioner of Police. Several users on Facebook inundated the picture with lewd remarks. Several men wrote that they wanted to be 'arrested by her'. Some even went to the extent of objectifying her physical features. A news portal even uploaded the video of her wedding to Dr Chris Abraham without her consent. Merin, however, took all this in her stride and used the social media following to help build the public's faith in the police and also spread the word about the need for more women in the force.

After the first spate of sexist trolling, Merin became a subject of several newspaper articles. A leading national daily that interviewed her after she had taken charge as Assistant Superintendent of Police under training in Ernakulam Rural District in 2014, mentioned that she had 'soft hands' and while talking to them had her 'hair tied back'.[10] This was seen as most inappropriate by many feminist portals. One of them wrote: 'Vomiting at every sexist reference to Merin Joseph in the media would probably kill us.'[11]

While Merin resisted the urge to respond to the debate that had been sparked by the largely sexist reportage right from her days as a trainee, an article in a leading daily in 2016 titled '10 Most Beautiful IAS and IPS Officers in India' made her take to social media, where she wrote:

'This perfectly sums up what is wrong with the

---

[10]Menon, Anasuya, 'Pretty tough cop', *the hindu.com*, 21 June 2014, https://tinyurl.com/5d23hvxm. Accessed on 15 September 2025.

[11]Rajaram, Sneha, 'No we don't want to know what you think of IPS officer Merin Joseph's hands', *thenewsminute.com*, 26 June 2014, https://tinyurl.com/yvyyp6vv. Accessed on 15 September 2025.

press in India, especially the vernacular press. Shameless objectification of women and propagation of patriarchal structures, reducing a lady's worth to her face value. These are bold and brave officers working in the complex bureaucratic system in India, negotiating their way through the good, bad and ugly of our body politic—and here we have a list of officers whom people can ogle at. It's seriously disgusting, constricting and very demeaning to our identities as smart, intelligent self-made women. Have you ever wondered why we never see a list of the most handsome males in the IAS and IPS?'

An even more fitting response was when at the Independence Day parade of 2016, Merin was in command, making her the youngest officer from Kerala to achieve that distinction.

In the Deep

In August 2018, Kerala experienced one of its worst monsoons, with incessant rains devastating several homes and establishments. All districts of the state were placed on red alert and Government of India declared the floods a 'calamity of severe nature'. Between August 1 and 30, Kerala received 821 mm of rainfall as against a normal of 419.3 mm. The extreme rainfall came in two batches, from August 8 to 10 in northern Kerala and from August 15 to 17 in the southern part. The ensuing flood devastated all but one district of the state. These floods were recognized as one of the five major extreme flooding events in the world between 2015 and 2019—the hottest five-year period on record, according to the World Meteorological Organization (WMO). It was named Kerala's *nootandile pralayam* (flood of the century) that reportedly claimed nearly five hundred lives, and in one way or the other, affected over five million people. The swirling flood waters swallowed up homes, hospitals, schools and many other private and public buildings. It led to major airports being temporarily closed; and the tourism industry of one of the most favoured destinations in the country came to a standstill.

The situation necessitated one of the largest rescue and relief operations undertaken in Kerala. Forty helicopters, thirty-one other aircraft, hundred and eighty-two teams for rescue, eighteen medical teams of defence forces, ninety teams of the National Disaster Response Force (NDRF) and several companies of Central Armed Police Forces (CAPF) were pressed into service along with over five hundred boats and necessary rescue equipment.

For an operation of this size, the importance of the services of an efficient control room cannot be emphasized enough. The choice to man this nerve centre falls on the most efficient, dedicated and imaginative police officers. Merin was Superintendent of Police, Railways, at the time and was handpicked to helm the State Monitoring Cell (SMC) Control Room operating in the Secretariat and was, therefore, in the eye of the storm. The success of the efforts coming from so many diverse entities depended on a level-headed coordination by the SMC Control Room. As the most senior police official amidst representatives from the Army, Navy, Air Force, NDRF and revenue administration, Merin had a formidable responsibility to shoulder.

The tragedy of gigantic proportions that was unfolding all around Merin would have tested the nerves of even the most seasoned leaders. Most public officials involved in the rescue efforts, including those specializing in disaster management, had never grappled with a calamity of that magnitude. Over two million people had to flee their homes. All these displaced people had to be moved to relief camps. Not just human beings, but even the cattle they owned had to be moved to safe places. After securing their lives, food had to be provided for the people and the cattle. Procuring food, clothes, medicines and other vital supplies for lakhs of people, some in need of immediate medical attention, was a tall order by any standard. This was the state of affairs in thirteen out of fourteen districts of the state. Often in circumstances like this, many field-level functionaries need their morale to be boosted and their spirits to be kept in high gear. It falls upon the officials in the control room to maintain the morale of the district-level functionaries at a high benchmark.

Merin's immediate tasks included collecting details of persons trapped in various districts along with their location coordinates and passing it on to the respective police control rooms operating in the flood-hit districts. These details would then be transmitted to the rescue teams operating in the field and carrying out rescue efforts using boats and helicopters. In cases of dire emergency, she passed on details of the trapped people directly to the Naval Squadron Leader present in the control room for urgent evacuation by air-lifting. In addition, she collected details from officers on the ground regarding their pressing requirements like fuel for the boats and medicines needed in the relief camps. This information was then passed on by her to the officer in charge of the Logistics Cell and followed up till the issue was resolved on the ground.

Once the victims had been evacuated to relief camps, the greater challenge presented itself—ensuring adequate supplies of food and essential items in the camps. Merin ensured that supplies being collected by various agencies and individuals were reaching the places where they were most required. Every day, she would attend the meeting convened by the chief minister and brief her senior officers with statistics on the prevailing situation.

&

'Ma'am, there's a call from Oman from someone who wants to speak to the officer in-charge of the control room. He says it's urgent,' the operator on duty informed Merin.

'Okay, put him on the line. I'll speak to him,' Merin responded.

The caller from Oman introduced himself as Wasim. He said he belonged to Chengannur in the Alappuzha district. 'Madam, I am working in Oman. My old mother lives in our ancestral house. Her name is Huma. She is paraplegic and has to move about on wheelchair with assistance from a servant. I keep in touch with her, and she always responds when I call on her mobile phone. But for almost twenty-four hours, she has not picked up my calls. I have seen visuals of the floods on television, and I fear the worst. Please help me.'

Merin assured Wasim that every possible effort will be made to locate Huma. She asked him to provide all the details he could—address, mobile number, father's name.

'Madam, my father died last year. Mother is all by

herself. You must be aware that Chengannur has a large population of the elderly whose children like me have moved out to seek greener pastures. I feel so helpless. I should have brought Mother here with me.' Wasim's words were punctuated with sobs.

'Compose yourself, Wasim. We have been inundated with similar calls from the US, Canada, UK and many countries in West Asia. In quite a few cases, we have been able to extend help. In other cases, our teams are doing their best. Don't worry, we will leave no stone unturned to search for your mother,' were Merin's reassuring words.

Merin asked the naval officer assisting her to send a message to the helicopter team close to the village whose coordinates had been found on the geographical map, while she was still on the call with Wasim. She also gave Huma's mobile phone number to her operator to pass it on to the cyber team to find the location of Huma's mobile phone. The police outpost was also given a message to fan out to see if any old woman had been located in the general area. Every few minutes, she was getting feedback from these three agencies. After about an hour, she got a message from the cyber team about the last location of the mobile phone Huma was using. It was reported that the last time there was a signal on it was about forty-five minutes earlier. Merin shared the location with the helicopter team and the local police outpost. They immediately swung into action. Close to the spot reported by the cyber team, the helicopter navigator noticed through his binoculars that next to a tree, there was a woman lying on the ground, seemingly unconscious. The spot was surrounded by flood waters. The information was given to Merin who directed the police to move to the spot where the woman was lying marooned. About fifteen minutes later, the police team reached the spot in a boat. The woman was located by them and they found her mobile phone lying a couple of metres away from her. The phone was lifeless. It was wet and the battery had also died. The woman was picked up and taken to the nearest relief camp where a medical team was available. After a couple of injections and other treatment, the woman regained consciousness. Then she identified herself as Huma. This information was conveyed to the monitoring room where Merin received it with great satisfaction.

When Merin informed Wasim about the rescue of his mother, he was hugely relieved and started to cry due to the sudden release of pent-up tension. 'Madam,' he said, 'you have done me a favour I will never forget. I will never be able to repay you but rest assured, I will pray to Allah that you achieve all that you want in your life.'

'What I did was my duty. I will try that you have a word with your mother. Her phone is not working. You will receive the call from some other number. Best of luck!'

'Thank you, *Khuda hafiz* (May God protect you), Madam.'

Merin instructed the officer in-charge of the outpost to arrange for the call she had promised Wasim.

There were many more cases of lost people from all over, and Merin and her team spared no efforts in locating them. As she made a silent assessment of what had been achieved during the crisis, she had every reason to be satisfied.

Just five years into service, Merin came up to the expectation of the chief minister of the state and senior functionaries of the government and police hierarchy. As recognition of the commendable work done, Merin was awarded a citation by the chief minister. To cap this recognition of the exceptional services she had rendered, she was chosen to command a state-level parade for honouring the members of the uniformed forces who had worked tirelessly during the floods.

∞

As she reflected on all these achievements, Merin recalled the harrowing time she endured during her training, a time that had made her question her decision to join a brawny service such as police—the time when she sat by the wayside during the forty-two-kilometre route march, all fagged out and in rock-bottom spirits. Now, she thanked her training programme which had made her physically and mentally strong enough to endure challenges that came her way. The lessons in leadership, the significance of working in a team with members drawn from differing backgrounds, were invaluable. Above all, her belief in her own abilities was now sky-high. If she could come out on top of the most trying circumstances of the 2018 monsoon, she could be rest assured in the belief that there was no challenge too big for her to overcome.

A Cold Trail

In 2019, Merin was posted to Kollam City as Commissioner of Police. Kollam is located on the southern tip of the Malabar Coast and on the banks of the Ashtamudi Lake. An ancient seaport, Kollam has enjoyed a strong commercial reputation for millennia. The Arabs, Phoenicians, Chinese, Ethiopians, Syrians, Jews, Chaldeans and Romans have all engaged in trade at the port of Kollam. Kollam has a large population of fisher folk from the Christian and Hindu communities. It is home to one of the seven churches established by St Thomas as well as one of the mosques believed to be founded by Malik Deenar. It is one of the fastest-growing cities in the world. The district poses a diverse set of challenges for the police—labour unrest, student politics and caste/community interfaces, to name a few. The district is also a political hotbed. It is a stronghold for the CPI(M)—Communist Party of India (Marxist), which faces some competition from the CPI—Communist Party of India, and local parties like the RSP—Revolutionary Socialist Party. The Sree Narayana College is the epicentre of student politics in Kollam and agitations stemming from political factions in the college often give rise to law-and-order issues. Kollam is also the headquarters of SNDP—Sree Narayana Dharma Paripalana Yogam—a social service organization that represents the Hindu Ezhava community since 1903. The Karunagapally municipality has a strong Muslim presence. This is also the area which houses several banned PFI[12] activists. Kollam is known for cashew processing and coir manufacturing. It is also a hub for marine exports. The Kerala Minerals and Metals Limited (KMML) and Indian Rare Earths Limited (IREL) are two vital installations in Kollam whose mining activities are often resisted by locals.

When Merin joined as Commissioner of the district, she was aware of the wide scope of challenges that the posting offered. As was her practice, she requested to be briefed, apart from the ongoing matters, about cold cases. Merin had three and a half months before she left for a Master's in Public Policy at the University of Oxford.

'I can't believe files about such dire crimes have been gathering dust.' Merin told her Reader[13] while going through the cold cases.

'Ma'am, there is so much workload. It is difficult to deal with every case.'

---

[12]Popular Front of India (PFI), a controversial Muslim group. Government of India has banned PFI for five years for allegedly having links with terror groups.

[13]Officer in charge of maintaining records in the office of Commissioner of Police.

'I understand but difficulty comes with our job. These criminals are still out there, and we must accept a part of the blame for that being the case.'

The Reader did not know how to respond and kept mum.

'I had asked for the files which pertain to crimes against women and children separately.'

'Yes, Ma'am. They are kept in the heap to your left.'

Merin signalled the Reader to leave.

As Merin started going through the files of crimes against children registered under the POCSO Act, she chanced upon Pooja's case. As she read through the Investigating Officer's (IO) report, she could not believe the degree of injustice the young girl's family had faced. She called the Reader back to her office and asked him to send for the IO of the case immediately.

'Why are we sleeping on this matter? The girl has taken her own life and so has her stepfather. Can you even begin to imagine the plight of the family?' Merin asked, visibly irritated.

'Sir... I mean... Ma'am...the accused...' the IO, Vidhyadharan, mumbled.

'I know the accused is in Saudi. I also see here that a red corner notice has been issued. What happened next?'

'Ma'am...there was no response from Saudi.'

'Did we try again?'

'No, Ma'am.'

'Years have passed. Oh my god!'

'Ma'am, no rape accused has ever been brought back to India from a foreign country.'

'Does that mean this one will also escape the long arms of the law? I will nab Satheesh. I don't know how but I will.'

Vidhyadharan struggled to find a response to what he thought was an impossible assertion.

'Also, isn't this girl, Pooja, from the Thandan community? And the accused, Satheesh, from the Ezhava community?'

'Yes, Ma'am.'

'I see from the report that the accused knew the family well. Then why haven't we added the SC/ST Act to the FIR?'

'Ma'am... I will have to check. Perhaps caste was not seen as a factor in this case.' Vidhyadharan sounded flummoxed.

'Caste is always a factor in our part of the world. Also, don't you know that the mere knowledge of the caste of the victim is enough to get a conviction. We must charge Satheesh under this Act too. Now, accompany me to the international crime desk.'

All the IO could manage in response was a faint nod.

Merin was determined to bring a change even in the short time before she was to leave for higher education. She knew that crimes against women and children, particularly those belonging to marginalized communities, had to be given priority, and in this context, getting Satheesh back to India would act as a potential deterrent for many a criminal, particularly those who thought that getting off on a rape charge was as easy as booking a flight to another country.

❧

'What is the step-by-step procedure for extradition that we have to follow in the case?' Merin asked Nair, the officer who was on the international crime desk of the district.

Nair mumbled without any visible confidence, 'Sir... Madam...we need clearances from the government. INTERPOL is already in the picture; we will have to follow up with them on the red corner notice issued in 2017. CBI (Central Bureau of Investigation) will also play a role. It is still a long procedure, Madam. I will have to find out more because such an extradition has never been done before.'

'What do you mean? Clearances from which government, ours or Saudi's?'

'I mean Kerala government first. A team has to go to the foreign country to get the culprit from there. This team will need clearance from Kerala government to travel overseas.'

'What is next?'

'Madam, we will first need to touch base with INTERPOL about the red corner notice. That will be required for the arrest of the accused in Saudi.'

'What else?'

'Once the accused has been detained, we will have to send a team to Riyadh to take his custody and bring him here for further action.'

'How will we approach the Saudi-based INTERPOL office to act?'

'We will have to go through CBI which has a dedicated unit for the matters of extradition, Madam.'

Merin turned to Vidhyadharan, who was sitting quietly in a chair and nodding his head every time the commissioner gave some instruction to Nair, as if they were instructions from him being conveyed by the boss. She told him, 'Vidhyadharan, immediately shake yourself out of slumber.' The brusque manner in which this was said shook the officer out of any indifference he might have had in the old case, and he became all ears to what was being said, 'Follow up on the red corner notice so that we may push for early arrest in Saudi by INTERPOL.'

'Yes, Madam. I will not lose any more time and quickly get down to business.'

'Vidhyadharan, I will watch you closely. Don't goof up.'

'And you, Nair, prepare a draft of a letter to be sent to the DGP (Director General of Police) for onward transmission to CBI from his office. You have been sleeping over this old case, of rape of a minor girl leading to her tragic suicide. This is an instance of distressing inaction in an important case.' Merin had underlined the significance she attached to cases where a girl was the victim of crime.

Merin was disappointed that the level of know-how about the process to be followed in securing extradition was so poor. She, therefore, studied the law related to the matter thoroughly, and was relieved to find that an extradition treaty was signed in 2011 between India and the Republic of Saudi Arabia. She also read about the procedure to be followed for securing the custody of the accused.

As she dug deeper into the details of the case, what saddened Merin was the near-apathy that had marked the efforts of the police. It is common knowledge that the presence of the accused in a rape case is an absolute must; she wondered why previously adequate follow-up was not done after the issue of a lookout notice. INTERPOL was requested to put out a red corner notice which was issued after a few mails had been exchanged, but then the case was slowly forgotten—an example of how even important cases sometimes get neglected for lack of adequate supervision.

INTERPOL

'The Real Taste of India'... Ironically, this is a claim which no one is likely to find acceptable, certainly not those who love India. This was a claim made by the makers of Kingfisher beer. The brand's 2022 'Spread the Cheer' campaign marked Kingfisher celebrating the year as the 'Year of the Cheer'. Undoubtedly, many would agree that the frothy brew cheers up. However, the name 'Kingfisher' is also reminiscent of a forgettable chapter in the history of India Inc. The airline by that name was closed down in 2012. The then chairman of the company, Vijay Mallya, had allegedly over-reached, and was drowned in debts drawn from seventeen banks. According to information available in the public domain, at the end of 2009, Kingfisher Airlines owed a massive sum of ₹7,000 crore, a major part of which was allegedly siphoned off by Mallya to shell companies in Britain, Switzerland and Ireland. Furthermore, he also left staff underpaid and even unpaid when he couldn't meet the due amount. Kingfisher Airlines finally crashed in 2012, with its aircraft seized. The man associated with the philosophy of living life king-size, the owner of United Breweries, which was already an MNC business conglomerate, comprising over sixty companies, became a fugitive from justice. His net worth was reportedly a staggering $1 billion. For the economic offences which featured Vijay Mallya as the accused, there is still a long wait continuing—he is living in the comforts of a palatial house he owns in the UK, and still remains a fugitive.

Mallya did what fugitives from justice have often done—rush to safe havens. The former Rajya Sabha MP (Member of Parliament) saw the writing on the wall, and fled India in 2016. He moved to the UK where he enjoyed clout in high circles and owned a place fit for kings, in what is known to be one of the most enviable addresses—in Cornwall Terrace, London. The tycoon purchased the property for a whopping €20.4 million, approximately ₹180 crore. Incidentally, this is not the only mind-boggling real estate he owns; he is reportedly the owner of many properties across the globe—California, Cape Town, New York, apart from ones in India.

With Mallya being so well-connected and stinking wealthy, the road to his extradition to India for facing trials in the cases he is accused in, was always expected to be a difficult one. The fact is that Government of India had to legislate a new law to ensnare him. The Fugitive Economic Offenders Act was rolled out by the government in 2018 and it was this new law under which Vijay Mallya was labelled as the first fugitive economic offender of the nation. The protracted legal battle in the courts of the UK has yet to conclude in the form of the fugitive's arrest. In fact, as late as January 2024, teams of Enforcement Directorate, National Investigation Agency and CBI have reportedly visited London to expedite the process.

Mallya is not the only one; there are other well-known cases as well. Matters pertaining to Nirav Modi, Mehul Choksi and Lalit Modi have been among the oft-mentioned high-profile cases. All these, and a few more, are at various stages of investigation and prosecution, being carried out by Indian law-enforcing agencies, and have benefited from the laws that make extradition a tough act to perform. Clearly, extradition is not merely a word with a long spelling; it is also a protracted road which has red tapes of enormous lengths, complicated legal clauses and sub-clauses which seem to be unending, and call for dedicated work from the police and the entire government machinery charged with bringing offenders to justice.

The case of Dawood Ibrahim, the most wanted fugitive by the Indian justice system, who is still at large, illustrates the complications that come in the way of securing extradition. In 1993, India sent a request to the UAE for extraditing Dawood Ibrahim, wanted for the Mumbai serial blasts that he had masterminded the same year. However, Dubai did not respond positively to India's request. The UAE asserted that extradition is based on reciprocity, and that India had not responded as quickly to extradition requests for Indians wanted in

Dubai, including one V. Sitharaman, who was alleged to have embezzled 42 million dirhams (₹340 million) from a state-owned travel agency, and Ravji Bhai Pawar, a domestic servant who was accused of assaulting a family in the UAE. It is now widely reported that Dawood moved to Karachi in 2015 and given that India has no extradition relations with Pakistan, his return to India seems unlikely.

Among the agencies that have a role to play in the working of extradition laws, one is INTERPOL—International Criminal Police Organization—which came into being over a hundred years ago. The official website of INTERPOL calls it an inter-governmental organization having hundred and ninety-six member countries, and which helps police in all of them to work together with the objective to make the world a safer place. It adds: 'The very first initiatives to discuss extradition procedures, identification techniques and record keeping are still at the heart of our role today… Locating fugitives remains a core activity, biometrics have replaced paper fingerprints and our databases contain millions of global records of criminal data.' India became a member of INTERPOL on 15 October 1949.

INTERPOL has four major organs. The General Secretariat coordinates the day-to-day activities to fight a range of crimes. Run by the Secretary-General, it is staffed by both police and civilians. The headquarters is located in Lyon, a global complex for innovation in Singapore, and several satellite offices in different regions of the world. India falls in the Asia/South Pacific region.

The General Assembly is the governing body and to take decisions, it brings all countries together once a year.

In each country, an INTERPOL National Central Bureau (NCB) provides the central point of contact for the General Secretariat and other NCBs. An NCB is run by police officials of the concerned country and usually sits in the government ministry responsible for policing. In India, the NCB is located in New Delhi. The NCB connects national law enforcement with other countries and with the General Secretariat via a secure global police communications network called I-24/7. The Ministry of External Affairs, Government of India, is the nodal agency for the purposes of extradition.

NCBs are thus at the heart of INTERPOL and how it works. They share criminal data and intelligence to assist another country. Likewise, they seek the information needed from other NCBs to help investigate crime or criminals in their own country.

NCBs work with the following offices as part of their role in global investigations: the law enforcement agencies in their own country, other NCBs and Sub-Bureaus around the world, and the General Secretariat's offices worldwide. NCBs contribute national crime data to INTERPOL's global databases, and cooperate on cross-border investigations, operations and arrests.

The Command and Coordination Centre (CCC) is the first point of contact for any country in need of urgent assistance from the General Secretariat or from another country, and serves as the nerve centre of INTERPOL's daily operations. The CCC provides 24/7 service round the year from its three operations centres in Singapore, Lyon and Buenos Aires. Its staff can help national police across time zones and language barriers when seeking assistance. This can be, for example, to locate fugitives or carry out identity checks or database checks. Processes involving extradition are a prominent responsibility.

Fugitives pose a serious threat to public safety wherever their tentacles reach. They are mobile, and often travel between countries on stolen or fraudulent travel documents. They are highly opportunistic and frequently finance their continued evasion of the law through more criminal activities.

Sharing information about fugitives and bringing them to the country where they committed the crime has been a core function of INTERPOL since its creation. Today, in a world where travel is relatively easy and criminals manage to cross borders easily, this function assumes even greater importance. The agency's website says: 'The world only gets smaller; for fugitives there are no borders, and close international police cooperation has never been more crucial.'

One often comes across the term 'red corner notice' in news reports, like the one issued for Satheesh. It is one of the main tools for tracking fugitives. It is an alert which is sent to all countries to request to locate and provisionally arrest an individual pending extradition.

Operation INFRA (International Fugitive Round-up and Arrest) is designed to locate and arrest criminals who have fled their national jurisdiction. This is organized by INTERPOL and the operation focuses on serious cases like murder, child sexual abuse, people smuggling, fraud, corruption, drug trafficking, environmental crimes and money laundering. While the case for which extradition was sought by Merin falls in the category of heinous sexual offence which led to a suicide, the cases against Mallya, Modi and Choksi fall under fraud and money laundering.

❧

An 'extradition' offence is one that, under the laws of both contracting States, carries a sentence of imprisonment of at least one year; it excludes political offences but includes serious offences like murder, causing an explosion, terrorism, etc., as well as offences that are solely related to the fiscal system.

A person who is accused of having committed an offence is usually tried in the country where the offence was committed. Sometimes it so happens that the accused flees the country to evade facing a trial. In such a case, the process which is set in motion targeting the transfer of the wanted person to the country where the offence was said to have been committed from the country where the accused has fled, is called extradition.

The term 'extradition' originates from two Latin words: 'ex' meaning 'out' and 'tradium' meaning 'give up'. It is based on the Latin legal maxim *Aut dedere aut judicare*, meaning 'either extradite or prosecute'. Of the two states involved, one in which the offence was committed is called 'requesting state' and the one where the accused or convict has escaped to is called the 'requested state'.

For two countries to agree to a process of extradition, they should have a 'treaty' or an 'arrangement' to undertake such a process. The major difference between a treaty and an arrangement is similar to a written agreement and a verbal agreement, or a binding agreement and a non-binding agreement.

A treaty is generally founded on the principle of dual criminality—based on the laws in the two countries, a person who is a fugitive in India will also be treated as a fugitive in the country in which he/she seeks asylum.

As far as arrangements are concerned, the countries agree to assist mutually in 'legal procedures', even in the absence of any binding agreement.

If India has a treaty with country X, then country X will act upon the provisions included in the extradition treaty when a criminal flees from India to that country and effect arrest, detention and extradition through a specified process. However, in the case of an arrangement, it will depend on the laws of the requested state whether the wanted person is detained or not. If detained, he may be extradited as per the existing international regulations only.

India's success rate in having fugitives extradited is abysmally low—one in every three fugitives is being successfully extradited to India even though India has extradition treaties currently in force with only forty-eight countries and extradition arrangements with merely twelve. Moreover, there are eighteen countries that bar the extradition of own nationals despite bilateral extradition treaties. Saudi Arabia is one of these eighteen countries and reserves the right to refuse extradition in the case of Saudi nationals. Fortunately, Merin wanted to have an Indian national extradited.

Extradition procedures enumerated in the treaty between India and Saudi Arabia are as follows:

An extradition request under this Treaty shall be submitted in writing by the Central Authority of the Requesting Party to the Central Authority of the Requested Party through diplomatic channels. The extradition request shall be accompanied by the following documents:

1. A detailed statement of the identity of the person sought, his description, nationality and if possible his address in the requested State and photograph. The investigating police, in this case the one working under Merin, has the responsibility to collect and provide this information.
2. Arrest warrant against the person sought issued by the competent authority, a statement of the facts of the offence and punishment for which extradition is sought, the text of the relevant legal provisions, and sufficient evidence for the detention of the person sought for trial. The arrest warrant was issued after the Kollam district police approached the competent court. Likewise, a detailed account of the facts related

to the commission of the offence was furnished.

3. If the request relates to a person who is already convicted and sentenced, it shall also be accompanied by a certified copy of the conviction and sentence, a statement that the person is not entitled to question the conviction or sentence and showing how much of the sentence remains to be served. Thakshak Satheesh was not one in this category.

Provisional arrest has also been described as follows:

1. In urgent cases and upon request by the Competent Authority of the Requesting Party, the person sought may be provisionally arrested for the purpose of extradition, and temporarily detained until the receipt of a formal extradition request under this Treaty. The request for provisional arrest shall be submitted to the Competent Authority of the Requested Party through diplomatic channels or through the International Police (INTERPOL), or any other applicable means of communication.
2. The request for provisional arrest shall contain a description of the person sought—a statement that extradition is to be requested, a statement as to the existence of the warrant of arrest, a statement of the punishment that can be or has been imposed for the offence, including the time left to be served, and where known, the location of the person sought.
3. If a formal extradition request is not received within sixty days of the date of provisional arrest, the

person sought will be set free. This provision shall not prevent the institution of further proceedings for the extradition of the person sought if a request is subsequently received.

Central Authority:

1. All requests under this Treaty shall be received and submitted through the Central Authorities of the Parties.
2. For the Republic of India, Central Authority is the Ministry of External Affairs, and for the Kingdom of Saudi Arabia it is the INTERPOL Riyadh, Ministry of Interior.

To understand what challenges Merin and officers working under her command were up against, one has to only look at the poor record India has in this regard. At times the problems arise due to certain stipulations contained in the extradition treaty itself; at other times outside the treaty terms. For instance, Saudi Arabia does not extradite its own citizens to be tried in India. As mentioned earlier, fortunately, this was not the case in the extradition request for Satheesh.

Challenges to extradition orders can, at times, be raised outside treaty terms as well. These are generally based on concerns of human rights violations, such as cruel, inhuman and degrading treatment or torture in other ways. The extent to which foreign courts will inquire into these concerns depends on the judiciary's role in domestic justice systems, and the strength of the human rights movement in that country. European countries including the UK have been more stringent in rejecting extradition cases on human rights concerns, such as the possibility of receiving 'torture, inhuman and degrading treatment' at the hands of the requesting state. The significant importance given to human rights concerns has evolved as a result of effective individual rights movements in the European nations. The UK also has a policy to examine individual rights as can be seen from the extradition process which was followed in the case of Vijay Mallya. So much so that the London court hearing the final extradition case of Vijay Mallya has demanded video proof of the conditions in Arthur Road Jail. This was in response to Mallya earlier telling the court that he should not be extradited to India since the country's prisons were overcrowded and had poor hygiene. Mallya's lawyer told the court in December 2017 that the conditions at Barrack 12 of Arthur Road Jail, where Mallya would be held, were 'far from satisfactory'.

Extradition procedures are further delayed by the variance in documentary requirements prevailing in foreign countries. Once investigations are completed by the requesting state or central agencies, they forward a request containing full details of the case accompanied with translations (where required) detailing the offences charged with, witness testimonies, arrest warrant, and documents establishing the identity of the fugitive. These requests are received by the Consular, Passport and Visa

Division of Ministry of External Affairs (MEA), and are processed in consultation with the Legal and Treaties Division of the ministry. Irregularities that arise at this stage—delays in investigation, alleged misbehaviour by police officials, improper documents, and incorrect format of the affidavits and certificates submitted—may be noticed at the judicial review before the matter goes to foreign courts. Further, an inadequate or flawed understanding of the procedural laws and investigational ethos of foreign states cannot be ruled out. All these factors were at play when the documents were to be prepared by Kerala Police.

Delays in investigation retard the process of submitting extradition requests or invoking INTERPOL mechanisms like the red corner notice that help in locating and provisionally arresting offenders. For instance, no request for extradition has been received from investigation agencies for the return of Lalit Modi, former Chairman of the Indian Premier League (IPL), accused of financial irregularities in the tournament's 2009 season. According to news reports, there is no investigation underway in this high-profile case, and the question of filing a charge sheet in a court of law has not arisen.[14] In the case of Satheesh, while the investigation had been completed in a reasonable amount of time, the lack of follow-ups on the

[14]Das, Saurav, 'What the Union Government Has Done to Investigate the Charges Against Lalit Modi', *the wire.in*, 22 September 2023, https://tinyurl.com/3rtcykej. Accessed on 15 September 2025.

red corner notice had left the extradition in cold storage.

It needs to be understood that documentary and evidentiary requirements for extradition must comply not only with treaty conditions but also with domestic laws of the requested state. Unauthenticated documents and translations not certified by a sworn translator can create doubts regarding the veracity of allegations, and eventually lead to denial of extradition requests. For instance, in 2014, in the case of the extradition request for Frenchman Mathieu Nicolas Furic, who allegedly committed sexual offences with children in the state of Odisha, the Namibian High Court turned down India's request.

It is often said that the judicial process of extradition is peppered with political aspects that underlie the situation. When officials of the MEA forward a formal extradition request to its diplomatic counterparts of the requested state, the foreign government is ordinarily required to act on the request by issuing an extradition order. However, the alacrity exhibited by the concerned government often depends on bilateral relations. In some cases, it is even exploited as an opportunity to gain mileage in negotiations. The Netherlands government's response to initiate the extradition process for Neils Holck (aka 'Kim Davy') involved in the sensational 'Purulia Arms Drop Case' and charged with weapons smuggling in India was to ignore the request for eight years. This case was embroiled in cultural and political misunderstandings—factual discrepancies, potential human rights violations and apprehensions regarding India's true intentions for seeking extradition. For these reasons, the Netherlands appeared to be unwilling to process the request expeditiously.

Another much-talked-about case is the one related to the 1984 Bhopal Gas Tragedy. During investigations, it was revealed that the then CEO of Union Carbide, Warren Anderson, was aware of the untested technology, faulty design, and unsafe location of the lethal methyl isocyanate (MIC) gas in Bhopal's pesticide plant. A few days following the tragedy, Anderson visited Bhopal and was arrested by the authorities upon his arrival. However, he was soon released on bail allegedly on the directions of the Central Government, which, it was said, came under US pressure to do so. India requested Anderson's extradition from the US on the basis of the criminal charges in May 2003, nearly two decades after the tragedy. The US declined the extradition request on the grounds that it did not fulfil all conditions laid down in the India-US extradition treaty, the alleged lack of evidence being one. It is believed that the US was reluctant to impose criminal liability for a case that was seen as a civil liability issue. The US wanted to avoid creating a precedent for cases against heads of American multinational corporations in similar circumstances if and when they arose.

Getting Thakshak Satheesh back to India to face a trial for his misdeeds was a tall order—one that Merin accepted even though she had limited time to pull it off. The long process of extradition is one that often demoralizes investigating and prosecuting agencies. In this regard, Merin's ability to feel the pain the victim had endured brought to the fore her tenacious mettle. Her empathy for the victim and her loved ones led to a greater commitment to bring the wrongdoer to justice, different from the usual detached approach seen in many other law-keepers. Pooja's case was one in which the victim was a young girl short of adulthood in years and who belonged to a scheduled caste—both served as factors that made Merin even more determined to have Satheesh extradited, and bring him to justice.

The Arrest

Captain Habib, the stocky station in-charge of the central police station of Riyadh, was trying his best to concentrate on the orders which had arrived a few hours earlier from the district police headquarters. He was unable to make any sense of what had been written. He muttered under his breath, and was in a foul mood even by his standards—standards that bordered on the unacceptable at most times, even more so when he was dealing with his junior colleagues, whom he considered fit for unapologetic disdain. He would also be on the brink when he was forced to read a text. He was a man of the field, a man of action, and by and large a competent cop. His failings often arose from the norms the Saudi society followed. He was contemptuous of the idea of human rights, and believed in summary action with the bare minimum pretence of a process of law when an accused was to be brought to justice. He also felt that bodies like Amnesty International were a hindrance in the dispensation of justice, and they had little idea what the real world was like.

The immediate cause for his discomfort was the order he had in front. It spoke of alleged discrimination against women in law and in practice, including in matters of marriage, divorce, child custody and inheritance in Saudi Arabia. The order was for police to be vigilant in this regard and to see that women received respect and fair treatment.

'Suleiman, come here,' Habib shouted. Suleiman was his favourite officer in whom he confided when he had to share his disagreement about orders received from higher-ups.

'Yes, Sir,' was the feeble response of the soft-spoken Suleiman.

'What's the problem with these Amnesty guys? Don't they have any useful business? Why do these people keep preaching to us? Let them treat their women the way they want to. Why are they telling us how we should treat ours? Suleiman, tell me, will you let your wife roam about freely without wearing the proper attire?'

'Sir, what's there in the order?'

'Nonsense and loads of muck. They want women to be treated at par with men! Just imagine the disruption this will cause in our society. They are accusing us of torture and other cruel, inhuman, or degrading treatment or punishment, and other abuses when we deal with under-trials and suspects. They are overlooking the fact that we have made Riyadh far safer than London, Paris or New York. Now will they tell us how to maintain peace in our country?' Habib looked livid, and his face was as red as a beetroot as he added, 'Suleiman, the time has come to understand that this human rights thing is going to cause mayhem; we must call out the fraud that it all is.'

All this while, Suleiman was nodding, indicating his complete agreement with whatever was being said by his boss. As if to confirm that he was equally uneasy with the winds of modern thinking, he said, 'Sir, I see doom for these countries. They are going to pay a heavy price for it all. We must not buckle under pressure of these so-called liberal ideas. We must abide by Sharia.'

A moment later, Khalil, the officer on duty at the wireless station, came with a sealed envelope. 'Sir, we have an encrypted message,' he informed Habib. Suleiman, who was sitting closer to where Khalil was standing, extended his hand to take the envelope. Khalil, however, did not hand over the message to him, saying, 'Sorry Sir, this is meant for the boss.'

Habib took the envelope from Khalil and picked up the paper knife kept on his immaculately arranged desk. With utmost care, he opened the envelope which had a large red stamp of 'Confidential' on it. A moment later, his eyes were glued to the text he had in front of him.

He signalled Khalil to leave. He showed the message to Suleiman. He read it twice before he looked at Habib, whose gaze was fixed on the face of his confidante.

'Sir, this case is again one in which we have to take action because wrong was supposedly done to a woman. I know that some of these Asian countries also have a soft corner for women and have an anti-male attitude,'

Suleiman spoke with an air of derision.

'Yes, this is from India. I am surprised that the authorities have this attitude there. I hope they will become wiser in future.' As he spoke, even the patriarchal Habib felt a sense of guilt about making light of Pooja's suffering. After a brief pause, he added, 'But this case is particularly gruesome. The bastard deserves the wrath of Allah.'

Both Habib and Suleiman fell silent for a bit, and were lost in their own thoughts. Habib had started his plans to take action to comply with the order. Suleiman was wondering what his boss was up to.

Minutes later, Habib had moved to an inner chamber at the station. There he had Hosam sitting across a small desk. The room was soundproof, yet Habib spoke in near whispers, 'Hosam, this is important. A man from India is here in Riyadh. He is wanted in a case of rape by the Indian police. We have to locate the man and take him into custody. Indian authorities will take him away.'

'Sir, how long do we have to do this work?'

'Not much time. INTERPOL will be associated in this work. In fact, the message we have here is from them.' Habib showed the message to Hosam.

After reading the message, Hosam said, 'Seems like looking for a needle in a haystack. There are a few thousand Indians working as menial labourers in Riyadh. This Thakshak Satheesh is probably one of them. He is from Clappana village of Kollam district. We only have sketchy information about him in this message. Even his photograph is old and not very clear.'

'Hosam, this is your responsibility. After all, you are the in-charge of intelligence regarding workers from South Asia. As you can see, the red corner notice was issued a couple of years back but there was no follow-up. I have heard that the authorities in India are a lot more proactive this time around. If you fail to locate this man, it will be an international embarrassment. Remember, I do not brook failure here. Understand this loud and clear. You have to deliver, or suffer the consequences if you do not.'

'But, Sir, the information is sparse as you can see.'

'No, I don't. All I know is that I have given you a task, and you have to deliver the results to me; and that too within the next two days. That is all, no extensions. I want Thash…eesh, or whatever the blighter's name is, in the next forty-eight hours. I hope you are clear about this.'

'Yes, Sir. I will do my best,' Hosam said feebly.

As he got up, Hosam looked unsure of himself. He collected a copy of the order from Habib before he left the office; signs of worry lined his forehead. He felt a tingling sensation in his right shoulder, something that happened with him when the going was rough and he foresaw failure at the end of a lot of effort.

In his own chamber, Hosam found no comfort in sitting down. He also felt his cervical pain shooting up when he walked around in his office nervously. The challenge ahead was one which appeared almost intractable to him—one man from India among several thousand working in Riyadh, his whereabouts inadequate and details sketchy. He wondered if he should go and tell Habib to find someone else to do the job. Habib's short timeline seemed devoid of the realization that the six states of the Gulf Cooperation Council (GCC)—Bahrain, Kuwait, Qatar, Oman, Saudi Arabia, and the United Arab Emirates (UAE)—are home to approximately ten million foreign workers, with the largest number in Saudi Arabia. He surmised that Habib was overlooking the fact that there were seven million expatriates in the kingdom, about one-third of the total population, and according to an official estimate, as far back as five years, there were 8.8 million foreigners in the kingdom, representing almost half the indigenous population.

Hosam also calculated the harm that not finding the Indian fugitive would cause. He knew that Habib was a ruthless boss, and he would not hesitate to take some unpleasant step, maybe even dismiss him. He recalled the fate of Shahid, the honest and hardworking intelligence official when he failed to predict a riot which broke out at a factory site. Shahid was summarily dismissed from service with the rider that he would never be employed again by the police force anywhere in the Kingdom. Hosam wondered if withdrawing from the search for Satheesh could lead to the end of his employment.

Just as Hosam was weighing his options, there was

a knock on the door. He opened it, and found Hasan al-Namlah standing there, looking cheerful as always. '*As salaam alaykum*' (Peace be upon you), Hasan said warmly, and they immediately hugged each other. Hosam responded with '*Marhaba* (Welcome), Hasan! Marhaba. Marhaba. I could not have asked for anything better... Hasan, you have come when I needed you the most. Marhaba again.'

Hosam and Hasan went back a long way. They were together in school at the primary level, and both worked for a career in the police. While Hosam made it to the elite intelligence wing, Hasan was in the executive police. The two were together for much of their careers, but Hasan decided to opt for a job in the oil sector as security advisor for a major oil production company, while Hosam continued with his job in Riyadh Police. Hosam was often approached by Hasan to take up an oil field security advisor's job, but the former enjoyed his job and spurned even those jobs where the pecuniary gains were handsome.

Today, when Hasan came, Hosam almost craved for a renewal of the offer his friend had made earlier. His own position appeared to be a bit shaky to Hosam, thanks to what Habib had asked him to do in the following two days.

Hasan and Hosam started reliving their days in the police. At one point Hasan said, 'Ho, sometimes I think what my life would have been like had I continued with the force. I envy you for your resilience in hanging on here even when very attractive offers to serve in the oil sector came to you. Today, I am in a secure job and have hardly any regrets for opting out of the police a few years ago. Yet, I must confess that the prestige and power that a job with Saudi Police carries is irreplaceable.'

'You are right, Ha (Ho and Ha were the shortened names with which they addressed each other, and they enjoyed being identified together as HoHa), I thought that the main reason why I continued with the police was because my stature in society was helped by this position. However, today I am wondering whether I might have been more comfortable in other jobs,' Hosam admitted to his friend.

Hasan was surprised to hear what his friend had just said, and made no secret of it. 'Don't tell me you are serious, Ho. I always admire you for the resolve you have shown in continuing with the police despite the challenges the job throws at you. Now you are telling me you have had a different take! Honestly, I don't believe you. Tell me why you are saying this. It's not like you.'

'You are right, Ha. I have been telling you all these years that I have no intention of leaving the force prematurely, but the pressure is sometimes too much for me to bear.'

'Ho, tell me in detail. I must know what is bothering my friend.'

'No, there's nothing that you will be able to help me with. Actually, a little while ago I have been asked to locate a worker from India who is working here in Riyadh. You know that the city has a huge number of Indian workers and not all of them are documented in our government records. The one I have been tasked to locate is a lowly menial worker, the details about whom are grossly inadequate. And I have been told that I have to find him in the next forty-eight hours. You know, I have had many successes of this nature in the past, but in this case the identity of the person is not well established in the records. I am at my wit's end.'

'I know you cannot tell me much for reasons of secrecy. But can you share at least some details? Maybe I will be able to help you.'

'Okay, I can tell you that the person we are looking for is from India. He comes from the state of Kerala. He is from the Clappana village of Kollam district. He is a Hindu, and is a lowly-placed worker in a road construction company. His name is Thakshak Satheesh.'

'A road construction company? Indian? Let me think…is he working for an Indian company or some American company, Ho?'

'The records are incomplete, so all I can do is make a guess—must be an Indian company. Just a hunch, mind you.'

'What's your hunch based on?'

'That's because he is from Kollam district of Kerala which has most of its Hindu workers employed in Indian companies.'

Hasan's eyes lit up, 'If your hunch is right, then possibly we can restrict our search to just two or three companies which have a majority of workers from Kollam. I know two Malayalis who own road construction companies, and they may be of help in locating our man.'

'Are they men of your confidence, Ha? We can't take a chance. A leak of what we are up to will alert the fugitive and we will find it hard to explain.'

'Yes, I have faith that I have made an accurate reading of these Keralite gentlemen. For them my friendship matters because I have a say in the success or otherwise of their ventures. Allah is *mehrban* (merciful),' Hasan asserted confidently.

Unni Narayana Menon was watching a movie in his home theatre starring his favourite heroine Manju Warrier. His devotion to the actress was doubled after she gained superstardom having starred opposite Mohanlal in *Aaraam Thampuran* (1997). In the film she played the role of Unnimaya who is the love interest of the hero. Her charm was something that had made a strong impact on the then teenager Unni. Whenever he had the time, he chose to watch movies, many of them starring Manju Warrier.

Hasan entered Unni's room unannounced while he was immersed in the movie; such was the closeness the two enjoyed. 'Sorry to disturb you when you are watching your favourite star, but I took a chance. I hope you have some time for me too,' Hasan said to Unni.

Unni, who was used to similar unannounced visits by Hasan, was not surprised. There was informality in their relationship, and either of them had the freedom to similarly barge into private time of the other.

'No…not at all, Hasan. It is always a pleasure to meet you. I was, in fact, thinking of you today because I want your help in securing some work from the city administration.'

'I know we have telepathy, and we often think of each other on the same days.'

Both of them laughed.

'Okay, Hasan, tell me what was the matter that made you think of me?'

'No, first you tell me, Unni.'

'My work is usual business—winning the bid for a hundred-kilometre road which has been tendered by the city administration. With your contacts in the council, I can hope to get a favourable response. You helped me earlier as well.'

'Not a big deal. I will find out if Mustafa can wield his influence in this matter. Otherwise I can ask Wahab as well.'

'Yes, they are both influential and can surely help. Now tell me, what has brought you here today.'

'Unni, it's a bit tricky. I am looking for a menial worker from your Kollam district who is working here in the city with a road construction company. I do not have a lot of details about this man's identity or current employment status. I know there are several thousand workers here and finding this man is not going to be easy. But I am hoping that you can help me.'

'Hmmm…what are the details we have?'

'Sketchy, at best. We have a photograph and an

incomplete address of the place where he is employed. We only have a vague idea about the place where he is living. His address back in the village in Kerala is known precisely.'

'Let me fix a meeting with the owners of two other companies, maybe having more than a solitary brain will make the riddle easier to crack,' Unni suggested.

Hasan took no time to respond, 'No, Unni. We cannot bring too many people into this. I have a commitment to keep it watertight. No leakage is acceptable. Our concern is to not let even a hint reach the target that we are after him.'

Unni thought for several minutes before he spoke next, 'Okay, let's keep it to us. Let's go to my office and have a look at the list of probables.'

In the plush office where Unni worked, the computer monitors were large and the efficiency of the touchscreen facility was on display. The search was on in full swing for the following hour and at the end of it, a list of nearly four dozen names was printed to be shared with Hosam. Unni had no idea what Hasan would do with the list.

The next stop for Hasan was Hosam's office. It was late in the evening, close to midnight, but the intelligence official was trying his best to make the maximum sense of whatever little information he had.

Hasan's list gave much hope to Hosam, and he dived into the system to work on the names he got from his friend.

'Ha, I am going to match the list you have brought

with the information I have. I hope we will be able to get to the target. Now it's late. Please go and rest. We may have to work a lot tomorrow.'

'Yes, Ho, I must go. But do not hesitate to call me at any hour if you feel that I can be of some help.'

The two hugged, and smiled, but the concern on both the faces was not masked by the smiles.

Hasan could not forget the tense and worried look Hosam's usually cheerful visage sported when he left the latter's office. As he drove back home, en route he decided to meet Mohan Vasudevan Nair, a close friend like Unni and employed as the HR head of a construction company specializing in city roads. His equation with Mohan was not as close as that with Unni, yet he decided to drop in without notice. Mohan, who was single, lived alone in a large house.

As Hasan rolled into the driveway, he could see that the light of the front room where Mohan usually received his guests was switched on. Mohan was very particular that unnecessary expenditure should be curbed, and was almost paranoid about conserving electricity. This was an indication that Mohan was awake.

To his surprise, Hasan found that the front door was not bolted and he could walk in without ringing the bell. As Hasan entered, he saw his friend sitting in front of a computer, immersed in some work.

'Hello, Mohan. I am here to trouble you.'

Mohan was a bit startled to be suddenly addressed from close quarters.

'Oh Hasan! What a surprise. I presume there is an urgent matter.'

'I know it's an odd hour to drop in. Yes, I have some urgency in the work that I am going to request you for.'

'Still, I would have expected a call from you before coming at this hour. In fact, I am preparing a presentation for a high-profile client. I was banking on tonight to do the job.'

'I am genuinely sorry for this intrusion. I don't intend to rob a busy man like you of the time that is available. I will take very little time to tell you why I am here, Mohan. You may decide the priority of the task I have for you.'

Hasan gave all the details he had about the fugitive that Riyadh Police was looking for. He also conveyed to him why it was necessary to act fast. Mohan understood that Hasan was in pressing need and decided to extend help.

'I think I have a clear picture of how we should go about this work. I am an HR guy, and almost all those who recruit manpower from Kerala come to me for consultations. I have a large data bank and I can dig into it for your purposes. Just give me time till the morning.'

'I'll not hang around. I want to leave so that you can get down to work straightaway.'

'Thank you, Hasan. I will now work through the night. Let's hope there is a breakthrough by the morning.'

∞

An optimistic outlook now replaced the distress which had filled Hasan's mind-space a couple of hours ago. The two friends Unni and Mohan had given him reasons to be hopeful. While none had displayed complete confidence, there was enough reason for Hasan to believe that at least one of them would deliver the much-needed information in a few hours.

Hasan called Hosam to tell him about the progress that had been made. Hosam also gave him a heads-up on the latest developments at his end. The tone of their conversation was, by now, of two persons who were reasonably confident of success.

Early next morning, Hasan received a call from Hosam. Although Hasan was very sleepy and had the immediate urge to reject the call, he knew that Hosam would be calling only because there was a genuine need to. In a drowsy voice, Hasan said, 'Hello. Yes, Ho, what is it now?'

'I am sorry to have disturbed you so early. But after thinking over the matter for the last couple of hours, I am of the view that we should form a close group of the two of us and your friends Unni and Mohan. We can together synergize our efforts.'

'You mean we should create an online group?'

'No, I want to sit with all of you and brainstorm on the matter.'

'Okay, I'll ask them if they are up to interacting with an intelligence official in this matter. They will possibly not like to be identified with the work of the police, especially when someone from their own is to be arrested.'

'I know, Ha. There can be sensitivity of this nature among his fellow Malayalis. I was thinking that you should not introduce me to them as one from the police. Let my official identity be kept under wraps.'

'That will not be right. Sooner or later, they will come to know and I will lose their trust forever.'

At this stage, Hosam saw no way out but to tell Hasan about the details of the detestable crime. As Hasan heard his friend, he felt a strong sense of empathy for the victim. A progressive thinker, he believed in the idea of gender parity.

'Let's be truthful. If they know about the crime this man has committed, they will be willing to cooperate. After all, he would bring a bad name to the entire community if he repeats an offence of a similar nature in this city,' Hosam said.

'No chance of that…he'll be hanged by the next electricity pole for everyone to see. The law is applied here with ruthlessness, and a long wait in handing out justice is not brooked.'

'So, Ha, can you give your friends an idea of the stakes involved without giving away much. You have to convince them to cooperate.'

'Okay, Ho. I'll talk to them and let you know the time when we meet.'

⁂

Hosam, Hasan, Unni and Mohan, four gentlemen with

personalities that had very little in common, were seated around a round table which Hasan used for meetings with his colleagues: one, a poker-faced, quintessentially withdrawn intelligence man with a restrained voice and studied expressions; another, an ex-cop with a certain degree of swagger and style; the third, pot-bellied and short, with a sense of humour which surfaced off and on even in times of serious conversations; and the fourth, a business-like executive with a sharp mind that missed nothing.

Hasan opened the conversation, 'We are all friends here. Let us not allow anything of what is shared to escape these four walls. Hosam is an old friend of mine from my police service days. He continued to serve the society and the nation by sticking to the job we joined together. He spurned offers to join the oil industry, and chose the hard life of a cop for himself.'

Unni got up from his seat and walked around the table to shake Hosam's hand. 'Sir, it is a pleasure to meet you. I admire your guts. But allow me to say that you look too gentlemanly to pass off as a cop…' His words died out as he understood that his comment might not be welcome to Hosam. However, the seasoned intelligence hand smiled faintly in response and nodded to acknowledge Unni's gesture.

Mohan extended his hand to meet Hosam's with the perfunctory, 'Hello, Sir. It's a pleasure to meet you.'

It was Hosam who opened the business part of the meeting. 'Friends, I am grateful to you for having found time to be here. My friend Hasan has been very kind in introducing me to the two of you. He has brought a lot of hope after what was a spell of pessimism. I am sure that with help from you we will be able to locate Thakshak Satheesh. He is the accused person in a horrible crime committed in India, and we must help the police there to bring this man to justice.'

'Yes indeed,' interjected Hasan, 'and the reason why the two of you are here is that the search is like looking for a needle in a haystack.'

Mohan spoke next. 'I have closely worked on my data, and have been able to identify seven men, one of whom could be the man we are looking for. They are from the Clappana village of Kollam district or nearby villages. These seven guys might be aware of the whereabouts of Satheesh. I think Hosam Sir might consider tapping these seven.' Mohan spoke with a lot of confidence which made both Hosam and Hasan look impressed, and they nodded their heads in appreciation.

'I have also looked into the data I have. My approach was two-fold. One was to concentrate on workers who have come from Clappana, same as what Mohan has done. The other was to look for such names which might figure in the column I maintain—one in which involvement in crime is recorded. Incidentally, I have seven names too which is a strange coincidence,' informed Unni, and added, 'Doesn't it look like the game of seven tiles we used to play as children?' The three men around the table did not react to the last bit, but were excited with the data which had been culled out.

The two lists were compared. The name of Thakshak Satheesh was not there. Of the seven names each, there were three common names. So the list of the persons to be approached narrowed down to eleven.

Hosam looked closely at both the lists and realized that the help he had from Unni and Mohan was invaluable. He was thankful to Hasan for his efforts. He spoke with much gratitude to all three, 'I don't have words to tell you how relieved I am on receiving these names. I now have at least some information which can form the foundation of the work we will undertake in the next few hours.' Saying so, he got up from his seat and hugged Unni, Mohan and Hasan one by one. 'Ha, I will never forget your help in this work. Allah will be mehrban and we will be successful. You have been an angel sent by Allah to help me.' Saying so, he once again embraced his friend.

❧

As Hosam drove back from the meeting, he made a stop-over at a shop owned by a Keralite. The owner Jamal Mustafa was a reliable contact for intelligence pertaining to workers from Kerala in Riyadh.

'As-salaam alaykum, Mustafa.'

Mustafa, who was busy with some calculations in a diary, looked up to see Hosam standing right in front of him. '*Ya Habibi* (Oh my beloved/dear), Hosam. What a pleasure to have you here right in the morning. To what do I owe this pleasant surprise?'

'Come inside, I want to talk in private.'

This was something which happened routinely. Hosam always wanted his conversations to be just between himself and his source of several years.

'But of course. Let's go in.'

Hosam gave a quick capsule of the matter that had brought him to Mustafa. He also showed him the list and asked him to make a photocopy.

'What do you want me to do with the list?'

'The usual stuff…just verify these names and their locations. Let me know as soon as you are through.'

'What's the time frame?'

'I am already running out of time. Take as little time as possible.'

'Okay, Hosam. I'll put my best boys on the job. Give me just two hours.'

'I will wait. May Allah be mehrban.'

'Khuda hafiz.'

An hour later, Hosam received a call from Mustafa. He gave three locations where pinpointed information could be gathered. He said that Hosam was sure to get Satheesh's location from one of the three names he had—Sreesanth, Aadinath and Kalappan. Their locations and phone numbers were also given.

Immediately after Mustafa hung up, there was a call from Unni. He said that he had found two possible sources that could be of help in locating Satheesh. The two names with locations were given, one of which matched the details of Kalappan which were furnished by Mustafa.

There was no intel from Mohan till this hour, and

Hosam thought that initiating action on the basis of available information was prudent rather than waiting for Mohan's inputs.

He, however, asked Hasan to speak to Mohan to find out from him if there was any information to be shared. About fifteen minutes later, Hasan called back to tell him that Mohan had suggested that recruitment agencies should be approached. He gave a couple of names too—'Alliance Recruitment Agency' and 'Wings Spreaders'. Hosam knew that the route suggested by Mohan was long-winded and time-consuming; and time was a commodity in short supply.

Hosam put two of his confidants on the job of verifying the information received from Mustafa and Unni through visits to the field. The reports corroborated the available inputs.

⁂

Habib was in a foul mood. He had spent the night working on the case and seemed to have hit a wall. His informants had asked for a week or more to come up with the information required for locating Thakshak Satheesh. This was too long a time in the hard taskmaster's estimate, and he was insisting on drawing a deadline not more than twenty-four hours ahead. He knew that his dependence on the intelligence wing was complete at this stage and, therefore, Hosam was key to the action that was to follow.

The sight of Hosam sitting across the table was a most welcome one for Habib. He was happy to see that the intelligence official was displaying confidence in his body language.

'So, Hosam. It seems we have something…do we?'

'Yes…and no. We have five locations and a few names. I also have a list of dormitories that house menial workers from Asia. Please have a look.' Saying so, Hosam handed over the dossier that he had prepared.

Habib took a long look at the report, and his facial expression showed that the accumulated tension was thawing away, being replaced by a relaxed visage.

'Why did you say no?'

'That's because I have not located Satheesh yet. We have credible information which has a strong likelihood of giving us the man though.'

Then Hosam made to get up and go. But Habib signalled him to sit down.

'Hosam, you have done a great job. I must admire you for it, but we still need to act on what you have brought here, then only the work will be over,' Habib pointed at the report he had in front.

'I think our protocol has been clear, Habib Sir. My work stops after intelligence collection; the rest is done by the executive force.'

'I agree, but in this case I want you by my side.'

'I should not be seen in the field. My identity needs to be protected.'

'I agree, you cannot be exposed, and there is no role for you in the raids except to provide information. But we need your astute guidance here. I will not ask you to accompany us on the raids but will expect you to be at hand in the control room. That will be useful for the field parties. I am calling Abdullah to finalize the teams for the raids. Please be present when Abdullah is here. That is an order.'

Lieutenant Abdullah, the tall, rugged and somewhat coarse head of the section dealing with force deployment for raids, especially in areas where South Asian labourers lived, was a no-nonsense cop. He believed in tough action, the meaning of which in his lexicon was to use brute force, sometimes touching on cruelty, especially when dealing with non-Muslim men and women who were reported to be involved in observing rituals associated with their religious beliefs. Intolerance of religious diversity in Saudi Arabia has been a known fact. Hindus are often targeted for possessing images of Hindu gods and for applying religious marks such as vermilion on the head (*tilak*). It is commonly felt that there is substantial prejudice against migrant workers, especially those from Asia and Africa. It was for this reason that any raid by the Saudi police sent a spine-chilling feel among the low-level workers.

Abdullah was the one to ask Habib about the task to be performed.

'We have to arrest a fugitive. He is from India, currently employed as a road construction worker. We know that such lowly paid labourers have no choice but to live in cloistered, over-crowded dormitory-type accommodation…' Habib briefed the Lieutenant.

'Serves them right, these blighters,' was what Abdullah mumbled under his breath.

'Abdullah, keep your opinions to yourself, I hate to be interrupted,' was Habib's stern response.

'And I hate these kafirs,' Abdullah could not restrain himself from spitting out these words.

Habib looked at him disapprovingly and said, 'Will you shut up, Abdullah? We have work here, not the time to discuss other issues howsoever important they might be.'

The beginning was anything but smooth, but Habib steered the discussion to become progressively more focused on the job at hand. Based on the intel from Hosam, he highlighted locations in Hara, Batha, Shamesi, Naseem and Malaz where Satheesh was likely to be living. The dormitories in these areas, where the majority of Hindu employees from Satheesh's home district lived, were closely studied by Habib and Abdullah through digital maps, expat records and lists available online from employment establishments dealing with South Asian recruits. Intriguingly, the name of Thakshak Satheesh was not found in the copious volumes that were combed threadbare by the officers.

In the absence of specific information related to the fugitive, it was decided that trial and error would be the way to move forward. Four of the five highlighted areas were shortlisted for conducting simultaneous raids. Batha was dropped from the list based on its high-end residents and business establishments. Five parties of twelve policemen, armed with revolvers and Sten guns in equal numbers, under the command of a sergeant were formed.

Lieutenant Abdullah was the first to address the parties. 'Listen carefully. You have been chosen to detain a criminal who has come to our holy land from India. He has to be caught because we do not tolerate criminals here. Get this despicable rat from whichever goddam hole he is hiding in. Through this action, we must give a clear signal that travels far and wide—we have no place for kafirs and criminals here. Make no mistake about this; I am closely watching each one of you. One stupid slip-up and your goose will be cooked. Don't come back with your heads hanging. I want my men to look proud and victorious. Now listen to what Captain Habib has to say, he is the one in command of all five parties. And we all know he tolerates no nonsense; he wants results. May Allah be with us.'

Habib got up to address the five formations that were neatly lined up in front of him. He looked even graver than he mostly did, which was in any case seriously grave. He panned the men standing from one end to the other till his gaze rested on Abdullah. 'Lieutenant Abdullah has given you a picture of what is expected of you in the next few hours. I endorse every word of what he has said. I must add that I will be severe if anyone of you makes a mistake.' After a pause, he continued, 'All the five parties led by sergeants will first reach Al Rajhi Mosque. From there, four parties will fan out one by one to Hara, Shamesi, Naseem and Malaz. We will use the Eastern Ring Branch Road for moving to our locations, which have been given to your leader sergeants. They are expected to tell you only after reaching the designated spot where you are going to be stationed. I will remain with one of the parties which is designated as the reserve party. Are there any doubts so far? Tell me when there is lack of clarity.' He moved to the front of the fifth party led by Sergeant Babar. 'Babar's party will be with me. This is the reserve party which will have twin purposes. It will be a cut-off party if the need arises, otherwise it will serve as the reserve party to be deployed depending on the situation.'

He moved back to the earlier position and said, 'On the way, the leader sergeants will give you all details they have been briefed about. We will move in five different vehicles, each adequately equipped for wireless communication and ammunition, should there be a need.' After a brief pause he ended his briefing with the words, 'We are Riyadh Police. We are not known to fail. And, Allah mehrban, we will succeed yet again. Let's march. Go to your designated vehicles now.'

Within minutes all the parties were in position. The party headed to Naseem had to make a little detour from the pre-planned route because the road was under repairs near Al Romansiah Restaurant. The four parties raided places of interest, but Thakshak Satheesh continued to be elusive even after a deep search of many dormitories and public places. Habib, who was with the reserve party, was getting frustrated, wondering if all the hard work would come to naught. He spoke to his colleague Sergeant Babar, 'Any ideas, Babar?' Even before Babar could respond, there was a message on the wireless walkie-talkie for Habib. Hosam wanted to speak to him on the cell phone.

'Yes Hosam, what's it?'

'Captain, I have a lead. This is solid. Our man is at the site where the repair is going on near Al Romansiah. There are about twelve workers, one of whom is Satheesh. Go get him.'

'That's pinpointed—the kind of information which brings success. I am rushing there. Tell Abdullah to keep party number three ready to help us should we need them.'

Two minutes later Habib, Babar and the rest of the detail had surrounded the construction party. Habib asked the person closest to him, 'Who is Thakshak Satheesh?'

In response, the person looked towards a person of average build. That was the indication Habib needed. He immediately drew his revolver and aimed at the person identified as Satheesh. He shouted, 'Hey, you bastard, Satheesh, surrender immediately, you are under arrest.'

While the man aimed at raised his hands in the air to indicate he was surrendering, he shouted back, 'I am not Satheesh, Sir.' As these words were uttered, another man standing behind him suddenly bolted and jumped over a road barrier, and started to run from the spot. Habib and some other policemen chased him. It seemed that

Satheesh had a lot of stamina and athletic abilities. He was able to enter a lane while the cops were in pursuit. Meanwhile, party number three also reached the scene and thwarted any progress of Satheesh. He ran back from the spot, only to find Habib towering over him as the deft move from another cop had made the escaping Satheesh fall on the curb.

'So your game is up!' As he said so, Habib gave him a painful kick in the guts. 'We don't tolerate criminals here. Go back to your country. If I could do it, I would give summary punishment to you. You don't deserve to live another day.'

He restrained the rest of the party from doing anything more and told them to take Satheesh to the vehicle, in which he was taken to the precinct's detention facility.

Red Tape

Two months had elapsed since Merin's intervention in the pursuit of Satheesh, when information arrived from INTERPOL that the fugitive had been detained in Riyadh. This news was certainly welcome, but there was a catch! This custody of Satheesh by the Saudi authorities was expiring in just fifteen days. The formalities for Merin's team to follow up on this information involved bureaucratic processes like clearance from the Kerala government to grant permission to the team to travel to Riyadh.

Merin had been interacting with her colleagues in the district about the process of extradition and had understood that if left to the IO and others, the intricacies of the procedure and the task of dealing with authorities of not just other countries but even the Indian officials at the embassy was too tough a challenge. She was wondering if she should lead the police party travelling to Riyadh herself. Before making up her mind firmly, she called an experienced officer, ACP (Additional Commissioner of Police) K. Joy, to seek his advice. Joy was the go-to person in many matters, owing to his long experience and a reputation for clear-headed thinking.

'Joy, you know we have to go to Saudi to fetch an accused from there. The extradition has reached this stage, and I am not sure if this last bit, that of taking Satheesh into our custody from that of the authorities at Riyadh, could be safely left to the IO and any other officer at that level. What do you say?'

'Madam, first of all I am so happy that you made the final push with such dedicated intensity. No fugitive has ever been successfully repatriated from Saudi Arabia. This is going to be historical. We must send our best team.'

'Yes, Joy. What is bothering me is that our know-how about extradition matters is not up to the mark. I was wondering if I should myself lead the team to Riyadh… is that a good idea?'

Joy responded as if he had been pricked by a pin, 'Madam, you? Really?'

'Yes, Joy. Why, is that not right?'

'No, I mean, yes! Well, I am thinking…you are planning to go yourself?' After a pause he continued, 'But Madam, dealing with the foreign authorities may be complicated. And, sometimes, the accused persons get nasty.'

'Come on, Joy. Are you suggesting I cannot handle a goon? If that's your impression, how do you think I will ever be seen as a capable police officer? Come to the point, should I send my name as the leader of the team for Riyadh?'

'Yes Madam, it's okay if you feel confident. But do think about the comments and other consequences if for some reason the mission fails,' Joy cautioned.

Joy shuffled away from Merin's office and headed straight to Nair's desk. 'Nair, do you know the CP is planning to head the team to fetch Satheesh from Riyadh?'

Nair was astonished. 'Do you mean that she is going?'

'Yes, that is what she told me,' Joy said with a chuckle, and added, 'Put some sense into her head. She is acting like a greenhorn.'

While this conversation was underway, there was a buzz on the intercom.

Nair looked at the number which was beeping and looked at Joy as he picked up the receiver, 'Yes, Madam.'

'She has called me.'

'I hope she has changed her mind,' Joy said.

As Nair entered the office of the CP, he found that she was looking at the honours board which carried names of all previous CPs of the district, apparently lost in her thoughts.

Merin was reflecting on what Joy had conveyed to her. She was pained to perceive an attitude in the seasoned colleague which underlined his reservations about her capabilities. He was suggesting that her lack of experience might be a handicap. It appeared to her that he was also wondering if a woman was strong enough to deal with a bully. In other words, did he see her gender as a disadvantage in her role as a police officer? If Joy had this attitude, could she console herself that he might be an exception and, as a rule, the others had an unbiased take on the matter? Or, is the advice genuinely meant to protect her from earning a probable negative assessment so early in her career?

She heard Nair approach, so she turned around and addressed him, 'Nair, a proposal has to be made for the government's clearance. We have to seek approval for our journey to Riyadh.' She found Nair gaping at her with an expression of inquiry. So she asked, 'Do you have a question on your mind?'

'No, Madam, but…I mean…well you said *our* journey…are you planning to go yourself?' Nair spoke with hesitation and in the process displayed his own wonderment at the advisability of the idea.

'Why, do you think I should not go?'

'Madam, it's your call…but it's risky to go.'

'Someone has to go. Someone must lead. I have not been able to grow enough confidence in the officers who are working on the case, owing to their inadequate knowledge in extradition matters. So I will go to guide them at every step lest some blunder leads to failure. The others will be ACP Anil Kumar and Inspector Prakash. Bring a letter addressed to the DGP (Director General of Police) for further transmission to the government.' Merin spoke with such firmness and resolve that Nair's idea of opposing her decision vanished into thin air.

∞

Later the same evening, Merin received a message that

the DIG (Deputy Inspector-General) wanted to speak to her. She could sense that the call was about her proposal to go to Riyadh.

'Merin, I find that you have planned to lead the team that has to go to Riyadh,' was the question that was shot by her immediate boss.

'Yes, Sir.'

'Are you sure? I mean is this a well-thought-out trip?'

'Yes, Sir. I have given it a deep thought.'

'I am wondering if this would be wise at all. You do not have any experience in handling a case of extradition. You have only recently joined as Commissioner so your knowledge of the case may also fall short of requirement,' was a clear expression of the boss's reservations.

'Sir, I have studied the case inside out. I am inspired to follow the trail to get the culprit to India. I want to see that he is brought to book.'

'Okay, if you are so confident and driven then I will forward the proposal to the DGP. Let us hope he agrees to send it to the government.'

Lokanath Behera, the DGP, had shown interest in the case earlier and Merin expected to get useful tips from him. So she called him.

'Sir, you are aware of the case in which we have to get accused Thakshak Satheesh extradited from Saudi Arabia. I have sent a proposal for a team to be permitted to travel to Riyadh and complete the process of bringing the culprit to justice in India.'

'Yes, I have seen the proposal forwarded by the DIG.

I find that you want to go yourself. Why so? You could have entrusted this work to some ACP.'

'Sir, I have thought deeply about it. I am eager to go and committed to seeing that the culprit receives severe punishment for his evil doing. I am passionate about justice for the innocent Dalit girl who was violated by this obnoxious man. And, Sir, you have always laid emphasis on the importance of international dimensions of investigation.'

'I am glad you are going with such high spirits. Best of luck to you and your team. I am going to speak to the home secretary for immediate permission. Of course, he has to get clearance from the CM (Pinarayi Vijayan). You have limited time, and there are a number of formalities pending.'

Two days passed, but nothing was heard from the government. Merin was worried that the delay may lead to failure. Of the available fifteen days, four had already been exhausted. Official travel abroad brings its own myriad preparations. In this case, after the Kerala government's approval, sanction for money, passports, visas, documents related to the crime and the identity of the accused were to be prepared. Correspondence with CBI and INTERPOL authorities was also called for.

An exasperated Merin got in touch with the DGP. The reassuring words of Behera were soothing as he told her that he will himself take up the matter with the CM.

'Sir, we have only ten days more. I am losing hope.'

'Keep all the papers that you have to prepare ready.

Make all other arrangements as well. Saudi Arabia being an Islamic country, you will have to use appropriate attire, preferably the burqa. So arrange for one. I am confident that we will get the government approval in a day or two.'

'Thank you, Sir. At my end, all the preparations are done. Papers are in place. I still have to arrange for a burqa though."

'Haha… I can't even say I want to see you wearing that garment; you will not be visible…haha!'

'I also wonder how it will feel to be behind the veil, Sir. I hope it does not feel oppressive. I will tell you about it on my return from Saudi.'

'Yes, keep your spirits high.'

It was at the eleventh hour that the Secretariat of the Kerala government appreciated the urgency of the matter, but not before repeated reminders from the police officers. The most shocking moment was when a functionary of the bureaucracy contacted Merin and said, 'It seems you are looking for an opportunity to have a free trip abroad. What is the need for you to go? You should leave this work to some other officer.'

Merin was piqued and felt like giving it back to the official talking so irresponsibly, but she controlled her vexation and coolly responded, 'Sir, I am a conscientious police officer. I have joined the police to serve the people, particularly the weak and the marginalized. Pooja, the victim of an evil violator, is at the centre of my thoughts. I am going to Riyadh to get justice for her. That is my duty, and I am confident that it is in the best interests of the success of this mission that I lead it.'

The officer at the other end continued to talk loosely. 'And if the mission doesn't succeed, don't forget that we will deem it to be your personal failure.'

'Sir, please wish my team well. We are going with the zeal of a mission; we need good wishes from all of you.'

'Okay, I will send it up for higher approvals. I hope the CM will take the decision which is in our best interests in the situation,' the officer said as he disconnected.

Meanwhile, the IO got the arrest warrant issued by the concerned court. Approval of the proposed names of the team was discussed at the bureaucratic level, and was sent to the CM after a day. The team needed the government's sanction for overseas travel. This seemingly routine action did not materialize before giving Merin some sleepless nights.

There was also the step of getting political clearance. This was at the government-to-government level, yet the passage of days over this process was taking away the precious little time there was. Issuance of official passports for the three officers to travel to Saudi Arabia was also dependent on the clearance. There was lack of clarity about the issuance of visa because it was understood that the team was travelling for government work on an urgent mission and visa would be issued on arrival.

Meanwhile, there was a linguistic barrier to be negotiated in dealing with the Riyadh-based INTERPOL office. Several emails were exchanged before this could be gone through to the complete satisfaction of all concerned.

The final formalities were accomplished only on the twelfth day of the fifteen that were available. The red tape had made Merin and her team walk on razor's edge.

Riyadh

'Faiza, I am so glad you are here. I want to ask you for a favour,' Merin said to her friend who lived in the Gulf, and who was visiting her family in Kollam.

'Come on, Merin! Are you joking? The police chief looking for help…beats me.'

'Listen, I need a burqa.'

'A burqa? Really? Are you operating incognito in some case? I am sure you are after a big-time gangster and planning a dramatic makeover to hide your identity.'

Merin laughed, and added, 'Are you seeing too many movies these days, Faiza?'

'Just joking… I know there must be something up your sleeve.'

'Let's meet.'

'Yes, do you want me to come over?'

'That will be great.'

'But I'll take a little fee…'

'A fee?'

'Yes, I would like to eat the delicious kebabs your cook makes.'

'No, not my cook, I am the one who makes them. Do you know, if I were not a cop I might have been a chef.'

'Now you must be joking! A chef…can't imagine you wearing the chef's long hat.'

'I am serious. Becoming a chef was actually an option I would have considered.'

'I must catch up with you on that. Will it be okay if I come over in the evening, Merin?'

'Perfect, Faiza. I'll serve your favourite kebabs as the fee.'

∞

Faiza arrived with a suitcase-full of options. The burqas had variety in terms of design, fabric and colour.

'Faiza, I find it amusing that the lady wants to hide herself, yet wants different designs and colours for the layers to cover herself from head to toe. Don't you also find it a bit odd?'

'Yes, indeed. You want to hide behind designer veils! That's funny,' Faiza laughed, and added, 'You know I have been to fashion shows in the Gulf where the latest innovations in burqas were on display. The models, invisible behind those yards, must be wondering about the impression their "looks" are making.'

Both the ladies laughed, and spoke almost together, 'Will the burqa fit?'

'Okay, let me try it,' Merin said and picked up one which had colourful floral embroidery done on a black background. She then had second thoughts and chose a black one with minimum embellishments.

'I think this nondescript one will be better for me.'

'Let me know the purpose, Merin. Must say I am intrigued that you are borrowing, of all things, a burqa. What are you up to?'

Merin slipped on the black burqa. Faiza helped her with the process. They both agreed that the fit was nearly perfect.

'You haven't answered, Merin. Why have you decided to wear a burqa?'

'I cannot divulge the details. All I can reveal is this—your burqa may turn out to be an accessory to an operation which will become an oft- repeated tale. Just wish me luck.'

'My best wishes are always with you. Please take any number of burqas you may need.'

'Thank you. You are generous, but only one will do. And now I am in a rush to pack, so let's quickly enjoy some kebabs.'

As Merin and her team finally boarded the flight to Riyadh, there was a sense of achievement as well as an understanding of how difficult it is to make the rusted wheels of bureaucracy move.

In the flight, Merin could not help but reflect on the way the colleagues in the department in which she served, the bureaucracy and possibly also the public at large perceived a woman as a cop. It seemed to her that gender bias was a reality which continued to dominate the perceptions about women in khaki even in the twenty-first century. This was particularly sad in a country where women IPS officers had been serving with distinction for forty years, shoulder to shoulder with their male colleagues.

Merin knew that if she was successful in carrying out the extradition within the remaining forty-eight hours, many of her colleagues would be forced to rethink their stance on women in the police force.

As the three members of the team comprising CP Merin Joseph, ACP Anil Kumar, and Inspector Prakash settled in their seats, there was a sense of great relief for all of them. Merin had the responsibility of leading the team. She had been through much tension in the past days and was experiencing a surreal moment—was she actually on the flight to Riyadh which appeared to be nothing more than a bleak possibility just a couple of days earlier? When Merin sifted through years of neglected records to identify criminal cases which had been overlooked for one reason or the other, she had set off a process which called for painstaking work. She had no idea that one such case would lead her to the Gulf on a mission to ensure justice done to a Dalit girl who was brutally violated, and who had been forced to end her life in a women's rehabilitation centre.

ACP Kumar was picked as a member to help the team with his hard-earned experience of serving long years in khaki. For him, being on the flight was a reiteration—a recognition of the consistency in performance of the arduous duties police officers render to society to give it a feeling of being secure. ACP Kumar was an investigator on the case when it was first registered and understood the intricacies of the law. He was puffed up to be on the flight and felt the enthusiasm of a newcomer because the duty to be performed was destined to be the subject of learning for many students of the science of policing.

Inspector Prakash had big boots to fill. He was on the flight in place of IO Vidhyadharan who was attending to a family emergency. While Prakash had responded to the calling by sifting through all the pieces of the story to give it a shape and undeniable meaning in his mind, he was still a bit nervous. As the flight began its ascent, he said a silent prayer to the Almighty—it was his first flight, and that too to an overseas destination. He was filled with child-like ardour—what will the foreign land be like? How will the people respond to him? Will they look at him with an attitude of piteous sympathy or will he be able to retain his usual composure? He could not overcome the fright which had surrounded his thoughts for being airborne at over thirty thousand feet. Adding to his nervousness were second thoughts about his degree of preparedness about the case.

ACP Kumar looked at the seat to his immediate left where Prakash was seated. He sensed something was bothering the man, who was at least two decades his junior in age.

'What is the matter, Prakash? You seem to be distressed.'

'No, it's alright, Sir.'

'But you don't look relaxed.'

'No, I am okay. Just a little unsettled.'

'Why, is this your first flight?'

'Yes, Sir. But that is okay. I was only wondering… I am several miles above the sea…'

'But that should not bother you at all. Aircraft have to fly at that height. There is nothing new about this flight.'

'No, just like that, Sir. It appears to be too high. Or is this normal?'

'Perfectly normal. The flights ascend to heights of thirty to forty-five thousand feet. So relax…this is no reason to be tense, Prakash.'

'Sir, I was also worried about being able to do the job for which we are going. I have never dealt with officers of foreign countries. Will I be able to understand their language? I hope they will not make fun of me.'

'Nobody will make fun of a competent police officer like you. They will admire your knowledge and efficiency. As for language, we will speak in English.'

The two officers had carried out their conversation in Malayalam and were completely comfortable communicating in their mother tongue.

'Sir, my command over English is not great. I can manage with a mix of Malayalam and English in my dealings, but in Riyadh I will face problems.'

'No worries. You have myself and Commissioner Madam with you. We will manage.'

'I am also feeling unsure because so many documents

have been asked for. I am hoping we have not missed out any. You know that I was the last one to join the team of sleuths.'

'Commissioner Madam has seen all the papers. She is meticulous. We should be sure about what we have given to INTERPOL.'

Merin, who was seated across the aisle to the left of the two officers, turned to look at them. She was happy to see that a continuous chatter was keeping them engaged. She had heard bits of the conversation, and was wondering if the nervous inspector needed to be given a pep talk. After a while, it was ACP Kumar who noticed that Merin had been taking interest in what he and Prakash had been saying. He smiled at her; the boss responded genially through her eyes.

Merin gestured to ACP Kumar to come across the aisle to have a word with her. She asked him about the state of Prakash's morale. She was disappointed to learn that the investigator was developing cold feet just hours away from the important mission. She asked ACP Kumar to take her seat, and she went to the seat next to the inspector.

'I learn from the ACP that you are a bit nervous. Is that right?'

'No, Ma'am, it's okay,' he replied and after a brief pause added, 'yes, Ma'am. My first flight.'

'Just that, or something else?'

'I hope I have not goofed up, that all the documents are in place. I am a bit nervous.'

'Come on, you are the backbone of our team. We are just hours away from performing a task which has become possible only because you have worked so hard in understanding all the evidence. In fact, we are more relaxed because we have your excellent memory to bank upon.'

'Ma'am, you are kind. But it is due to your leadership that we have come to this stage. I am just concerned because I have not been on the case for as long as my other colleagues have. I also know how hard Deputy SP Karunagapally, Shri Vidhyadharan, has worked in putting together the evidence. I don't want to let you all down.'

'You are in my team. There are other officers and men. My success depends on the team's performance. You are on this flight because you know your job well. Knowledge and competence are your strengths; you should be proud of your fellow officers' belief in your abilities.' After a pause she added, 'We have only a few hours to achieve success. The pressure is intense. Do you remember the famous dialogue of Shah Rukh Khan in the film *Chak De India*?'

'No, Ma'am. But I had liked the film.'

'Yes, as the coach of the team he tells the girls about the importance of being confident and giving everything they have to achieve success for the team. He speaks of the value of the *sattar minit* (seventy minutes) in a game of hockey to bring glory to the Indian team. Let us look at these few hours we are left with to get our man from Saudi as that short but memorable spell of time which we will look back on with great happiness and pride in the years to come. Trust your instincts, your hard work, training and competence; be assured that we will get the fugitive we are pursuing. "*Chak De India, Chak De Indian Police.*" It will be glory for us. Believe me, we are going to be four—three keepers of the law, and one who has broken the law. This team of three going to a foreign land will be returning with a prize. We will be victorious. Take it from me.' Saying so, Merin did a high-five with the colleague who was now a picture of optimism; Inspector Prakash looked the embodiment of what his name meant—brightness.

❧

Riyadh is the capital city of Saudi Arabia, an arid, sparsely populated kingdom in the Arabian Peninsula of the Middle East. Over the last two millennia, the country has seen several battles for domination. It was, however, as late as the twentieth century that the country known as the Kingdom of Saudi Arabia (KSA) took shape. In fact, it was in 1932 that two kingdoms, Hejaz and Nejd, came together to form KSA. Since this happened on September 23 that year, that date is observed as the Saudi National Day.

It has been said that Saudi Arabia is a young country which can boast of a rich history. In its western highlands, along the Red Sea, lies the Hejaz, which has Islam's holiest cities, Mecca and Medina. In the country's geographic heartland lies Najd, a vast arid zone that until not long ago was populated by nomadic tribes. To the east, along the Persian Gulf, are the country's abundant oil fields. This black gold has, since the 1960s, made Saudi Arabia one of the wealthiest countries in the world. These three factors—religion, tribalism, and untold wealth—have shaped the country's subsequent history. The fortunes of the capital city, Riyadh, which is home to seven million people, have also been accordingly fashioned.

Riyadh derives its name from the plural of the Arabic *rawdah* meaning 'meadow' or 'garden'. It is so called because of the abundance of verdant vegetation it has owing to its location—the juncture of Wadis Hanifah and Al-Batha. 'Few of the world's cities have transformed as rapidly as Riyadh, which grew from a small, fortified desert village in the 17th century into a modern metropolis of several million inhabitants in the 20th century.'[15]

Riyadh has the headquarters of a large number of banks, including Saudi Arabia's central bank. Being a financial, business and manufacturing centre, it has the offices of several private companies; in fact, every publicly quoted company is mandated by law to have an office in the city. One in three of the country's factories manufacturing machinery, equipment, metallurgical goods, food, chemicals, furniture, construction materials, textiles and publications, is located in Riyadh.

It is not difficult to imagine how frantic must be the pace in the city, but all work ceases, shops, factories,

---

[15]'Riyadh, national capital, Saudi Arabia', *britannica.com*, https://tinyurl.com/3zajv56z. Accessed on 15 September 2025.

every other thing comes to a stop five times a day when the prayers are offered. It is compulsory for all Muslims to offer namaz during the designated hours. The entire month of Ramzan is also devoted to religious activities, and little else happens.

There is practically no life beyond the official working hours. No night clubs, late night shows of entertainment, or anything that comes close to being called sun-downers or what may follow them.

The scene at the Riyadh airport was a familiar one—the hustle-bustle of an international airport, people hurrying all around, some lost, others swaggering around wearing the air of veteran travellers' confidence, stoic security men and shopkeepers at glittering shops—all pieces in their place that came together to present a perfect picture as it were.

But…look around, and something entirely unique was in evidence. It was the women; they were all wearing abayas or burqas, covered from head to toe. Their heads were also covered. However, it seemed that foreigners were an exception to this rule.

Merin was keen to observe the restrictions that Saudi Arabia, an Islamic country, places on the choice of attire that women wear in public places. By nature a disciplined person, she also looked at the plus side of wearing the attire which gave her anonymity. Ideally, not being seen as the odd one out in a public place suited the script of remaining as inconspicuous as possible. When she got out of the aircraft after it touched down in Riyadh, Merin was in Faiza's burqa. She had put it on in Dubai before boarding the connecting flight to Riyadh.

Wearing a strange ensemble was not exactly easy to accept for Merin, even though she had tried it on back home also. She donned the burqa with the apprehension that she would feel suffocated and that the heat of the Arab country would be unbearable behind those layers. It came as a surprise to her that her apprehensions were unfounded—the material of the attire was light, which negated the feeling of oppressive heat and there was no suffocation either. What helped greatly was the fact that there was little to be done away from air-conditioned areas.[16]

Strangely, there was a feeling of liberation. Her identity melted into the collective of many other women who were similarly dressed. She could pass off as just another woman in the crowd, and not as a senior police officer in pursuit of a heinous offender. She had followed her instinct in choosing her outfit though no one had told her before her departure that there was any compulsion

---

[16]'The time-honoured dress for women consists of a *thawb* beneath which is worn a loose-fitting pair of slacks known as a *sirwal*. In public women are expected to be fully veiled, and a long black cloak known as an *abayah* is worn. A veil called a *ḥijab* covers the head and another known as a *niqab* covers the face.' In 'Daily life and social customs', in 'Saudi Arabia' in 'Cultural Life', *britannica.com*, https://tinyurl.com/bdtcwpbk. Accessed on 15 September 2025.

in the Islamic country to remain veiled.

Women in public places of Saudi Arabia face discrimination which in other cultures would be rated as a human rights violation. A woman is looked down upon if she is seen talking to a man who is not her father or husband. Striking up a conversation with a stranger is therefore perilous, especially since the moral police, known as the Mutawwa'un[17], enforces strict codes of public behaviour, including gender segregation. Till 2018, women were not granted the license to drive cars. Once this restriction was lifted by the government, women could drive cars with the consent of their husband or father.

Merin had gathered knowledge about these facts before embarking on her trip to the Islamic kingdom. It was tricky for any lady police officer on duty to go in pursuit of a male criminal in association with male colleagues, in a setting where she had to refrain from interacting with other males. The conversations in public spaces had to be kept to a bare minimum in order to not have their cover blown.

---

[17]Mutawwa'un operates in plain clothes and enforces such Islamic precepts as ensuring that women are properly veiled, that shops close during prayer time, and that fast is kept during Ramadan. Imposing impromptu corporal punishment for infractions is an accepted part of its duty.

Lost in Translation

'Could I please speak to someone who deals with extradition?' Merin asked exasperatedly.

After several failed attempts, it had been possible to get someone on the line at the other end. The staff at the hotel was helpful, but language was proving to be a significant barrier. The communication skill of the operator on the hotel PBX was just about passable, and the effort to explain to him the need to speak to authorities in INTERPOL was an ordeal. When the call was finally put through, Merin could not be sure who was helming the receiver at the INTERPOL office.

'Arabic!' A gruff, unfriendly voice with a heavy Arabic accent exclaimed.

'No Arabic, only English,' Merin responded. She suddenly became aware of the wall against which her message was falling off and making no sense to the person with whom she needed to communicate desperately.

'Okay, let me speak to someone who knows English,' Merin pleaded.

'Only Arabic, please,' said the man who seemed

to have exhausted his entire vocabulary of the English language in that three-word sentence.

'God help me,' Merin sighed as she put down the receiver.

Her predicament was such that she could not have shared with the hotel staff the purpose of her attempted conversation with the authorities of INTERPOL in Riyadh. Only a handful of officials in Kerala Police and the CBI headquarters knew about the operation. To get her message interpreted by an outsider was too risky.

Once again, Merin tried to think of a way out while discussing with her colleagues ACP Anil Kumar and Inspector Prakash.

'Madam, let us go to the INTERPOL office. That's where we will be able to get assistance,' Prakash suggested.

ACP Kumar looked at Merin to assess her reaction to the inspector's suggestion. He wanted to be sure that what he suggested should not be shot down by his boss. The seasoned cop could make out from Merin's expression that she did not see merit in Prakash's idea.

'Madam, let us ask DGP Sir,' ACP Kumar's voice trailed off even as he spoke that short sentence. He thought that Merin might not agree to bring Kerala's top boss into the picture.

'Yes, the DGP has been very supportive right from the beginning. I think we can ask him to advise us. He has an intricate understanding of diplomacy,' was Merin's response.

ACP Kumar looked victoriously at Prakash from the

corner of his eye. He also allowed a faint smile with an evident air of superiority to slip through.

Moments later, DGP Behera was on the line, speaking in his calming voice, 'Merin, I think the CBI should be asked to help in this situation. Do you have a contact there?'

'Yes, Sir. The officer in CBI is Anuj Arya. He is of SP rank. I will speak to him.'

'Is he the one liaising with INTERPOL? Is he helpful?'

'Yes, Sir. He is forthcoming when asked to help.'

The time in Riyadh was about 2.30 in the afternoon, and Merin was aware that in Delhi the time for closing offices had arrived. She was keen to make headway immediately. Time was running out. It was the thirteenth of the fifteen days her team had to get on a flight back to India with the man they had set out to nab.

Merin placed a call to the CBI headquarters. As often happens in crunch situations, there was a message saying the line was busy. She called again after a couple of minutes. The number was engaged this time too. With each passing minute, Merin's tension was mounting. Thinking that ACP Kumar's phone might be luckier, she borrowed his mobile to make yet another call. This time the phone rang at the other end, but no one responded. Merin was now running out of patience, and said, 'Jesus, it's touch-and-go now! Come on, Anuj, pick up the phone.' She started to pace the floor frantically. She closed her eyes, and redialled. This time she heard the welcome voice she had been trying to reach at the other end.

'Hi Anuj, it's such a relief to know you are in office even though it's late,' Merin said with the confidence of someone who thought that the door to success had parted, even if it was just enough to put a toe inside.

'The Saudi INTERPOL officials speak only Arabic. They don't speak English, and here we are racing against time and running into this impediment of no communication. Help us. We have less than forty-eight hours left to get custody of the accused. Remove non-working hours from that,' Merin explained.

Anuj spoke with a sense of urgency, 'Merin, I know communication becomes a problem in some of these Middle Eastern countries. Why don't you ask our embassy to help?'

'Oh Anuj, you won't believe me if I tell you what the embassy has told us. They are not helping us at all!'

'But why? Aren't they there at the service of Government of India? Are they not feeling responsible that a hardened criminal ought to be extradited? After all, extradition is a long and tedious process. Now that you have achieved almost everything, why do they not understand the importance of this work?' The CBI officer sounded frustrated.

'The embassy told me that the Kerala government's letter did not "explicitly" state that they were supposed to assist us! They have not given us even the minimum logistical support. We have been left to our own devices. When I spoke to the Chancery, I was told to contact the Second Secretary Community Welfare. When I contacted him, he was irritated about being requested for help in a matter which was handled by another Second Secretary. He is from my batch, and I expected him to be forthcoming with the help I was seeking. Naturally, I spoke to him with great hope. I explained the critical nature of the situation to him.'

Anuj asked Merin to read the letter written by the Kerala government to the embassy. Having heard the contents, Anuj said, 'This letter should spur the embassy to extend all help. It beats me why there is such a negative response. So, what did your batchmate Reddy say?'

Merin let out a little chuckle to convey her sense of scoff. 'After I had spoken to Reddy, he came up with a reply after a pause. And it was a reply which was an example of why bureaucracy deserves the reputation it has. He repeated exactly what I had heard from the other embassy official, "Sorry, unless there is an explicit request to help you from your government, our hands are tied."'

'So, from one desk to the other, I was kicked around with no help. If I may say so, all the help I got from the embassy was when the ambassador posed with me for a photograph and asked if I would care for a cup of tea!' Merin managed to laugh at her own handicap.

'Okay. I will ask our Riyadh section in the INTERPOL branch to have a word with the authorities there. I have the details which you sent to the CBI about the case.' These words from the SP liaising with INTERPOL were the most reassuring Merin had heard in a long while.

∞

Anuj Arya, who was a recent addition to the country's ace sleuthing agency, CBI, prided himself on being thorough. He tolerated no departure from what he rated as essential benchmarks, be it in keeping the files, the tea that was served in his office or the order in which things were placed on his table.

The case of Thakshak Satheesh's extradition was among the first few cases he was saddled with. He had read the FIR in painstaking detail. He was still a 'greenhorn' at the Bureau and the rust that corrodes idealism had not slowed him down yet. Fuelling his quest for justice was also the nature of the crime and Merin's perceptible desperation. The gory details of Pooja's end felt very personal. He was determined to make a difference. A closure was only possible if he acted fast. He was now an integral part of the team that was involved in the extradition. He knew that the CBI had to do a lot of the talking and there was virtually no time to lose.

As the call from Merin ended, Anuj noticed that the file which had been placed last on his table was not in alignment with the side of the table. He straightened the file to his satisfaction and opened it to find the last noting related to the officer in-charge of the INTERPOL Saudi desk. He had taken ill and was not available in the office. Arya lunged for the intercom to reach an inspector in that section. After a long ring tone that went unanswered, he decided to walk to the section located down the corridor on the floor above. To his dismay, the inspector was not on his desk. The others in the office informed him that

Ibrahim Bashar, the inspector, had left only a few minutes earlier.

Anuj called Bashar on his cell phone. The first call was not answered. The second brought the unwelcome recorded message that the call was on waiting. The fact that the time available was limited made Anuj restive. He said to himself, 'Damn it, I say! Pick up the call, Bashar.'

Minutes later, Bashar called, 'Sir, I find you called. I'm sorry I missed it.'

'Yes, I was desperately trying to reach you,' Anuj snapped. 'Where are you? I found you left early today.'

'Sir, you are right. I left office as soon as it was 5 p.m. I am at Sarojini Nagar market with my family. Tomorrow is my anniversary and I wanted to do some shopping,' Bashar said apologetically.

Anuj was aware that Bashar had no reason to be apologetic for he had left his desk only at the office closing hour. 'No problem. Carry on. By the way, is it possible to contact someone in INTERPOL Riyadh? We need immediate assistance,' Anuj asked.

'Please tell me facts about the case. I will contact Ahmad Bilal or Muhammad Darvish, who are both helpful.'

Anuj was relieved to hear the inspector speak so confidently about his contacts in the Riyadh INTERPOL office.

'Listen, Bashar, you will understand that it will not be right to share such information on the phone. Can you come back to office?'

For a few agonizing moments, Bashar was silent and then said, 'Sir, I am not too far from office. Give me about half an hour. I will be there.'

For Anuj, the next thirty minutes passed like a whole lifetime. He traversed each square in his freshly tiled office innumerable times. The tension added to the fatigue and he eventually sat down. Unable to get his mind off the ticking clock, he decided to have a look at the file about Thakshak Satheesh's extradition. He wanted to identify all the relevant points which Bashar would need to convey the required message to INTERPOL at Riyadh.

Ibrahim Bashar strode into the office with a gait that assured Anuj that the inspector had grasped the gravity of the situation. He took little time in going through the routine of wishing his senior and requested to be filled in with the relevant details. Anuj had seen Bashar a number of times previously but only in passing. It was the first time that he was talking to the inspector while he could observe him closely. Bashar, he noticed, had an aquiline nose and a fair complexion with deep-set eyes on either side of a prominent nasal bridge. These features came from his Arabic bloodline. The slight stubble on his face made him look handsome, though his short height took away a bit from his attractiveness. He was known to be a jovial person in the office, and while he was intently paying attention to what Anuj was telling him, there was a faint yet perceptible smile on his lips. He was thorough in his work and enjoyed the reputation of being dedicated to his duty.

The crisp briefing from Anuj was all that Bashar needed, and within minutes he was on line with Ahmad Bilal at the Riyadh INTERPOL office.

'We need to complete the formalities within the next twenty-four hours. If we fail to do that, the accused walks away scot-free, and all the hard work done by Kerala Police will go to waste,' Bashar pleaded in fluent Arabic. 'Please understand that our team at Riyadh needs your assistance to complete all formalities as soon as possible. There is a communication barrier because none of the officers who have come to pick up Thakshak Satheesh can speak Arabic.'

All this while, Anuj was admiring the persuasive tone Bashar had employed and the apparent ease with which Arabic was being used for communication.

'Oh, great! Thank you. I am grateful for your assurance to help. Please ask for the services of an interpreter to facilitate conversation between you and the English-speaking Merin Joseph, Commissioner of Police. I am sending her phone number for you to contact her,' Bashar said. 'CBI and Kerala Police are grateful for your positive response.'

As Bashar hung up, Anuj could not stop himself from hugging him. 'Bashar, you have done a great job. Thank you for peeling away from your anniversary shopping to help.'

'Thank you, Sir. This is duty. I did what anyone else would have done in such a situation. I only hope that there will be no more glitches in Riyadh. Goodnight, Sir,'

Bashar turned to leave. As he held the door knob to get out of the office, Anuj called out, 'And Bashar, Happy Anniversary to you and your better half.'

'Thank you so much, Sir, *mehrbani* (kind of you),' Bashar replied.

⁂

Anuj redialled the number Merin had used to reach him to inform her about the breakthrough. After a couple of long rings, the call was received by ACP Anil Kumar.

'Madam has just left the room for some urgent work. I will ask her to call you when possible,' ACP Kumar told Anuj in his rich voice.

'Oho! Any idea how long will she be away?' Anuj became a bit anxious.

'I cannot say, Sir. She did not tell us. We will have to wait for her to return. Is there a message for her?'

'May I know who I'm speaking to?'

'Sir, I am ACP Anil Kumar of Kerala Police. I am with Merin Joseph Ma'am here in Riyadh for some work.'

'Okay, Mr Anil Kumar. I am Anuj Arya from CBI. Just let her know that we have been able to get through to INTERPOL in Riyadh. I have given her cell number to the INTERPOL officer dealing with the matter. He will get in touch with her shortly.'

'I hope it is positive news!' ACP Kumar asked in a concerned voice.

'But of course, officer. Your team is on the cusp of making history. The CBI is proud to assist you in this effort. I am available at odd hours too if any further need arises. Best of luck!'

'Thank you, Sir,' was ACP Kumar's genuine albeit short response.

⁂

Merin was at the Indian Embassy in Riyadh when back at the hotel her colleague ACP Anil Kumar had received the call from Anuj Arya. She was making yet another effort to get the embassy to respond positively to her request for help with the process of extradition. She met the ambassador again to ask for help. He was welcoming and over another cup of tea told her that he was happy that she had respected the traditions of Saudi Arabia and was attired in a burqa. The ambassador also gave her an assurance, 'You are here again. I can sense your urgency. We will help you to the extent officially possible. But we will not be able to go beyond what has been requested explicitly by the Kerala government. Please meet Rahul Reddy, our Second Secretary.'

Merin had already contacted Reddy earlier which had resulted in no headway. She came out of the embassy with her hopes even more deflated now. There was a call on her phone which she could not take while she was with the ambassador. It was from ACP Kumar. She called back.

'Ma'am, there was a call from Mr Anuj Arya. He wanted you to contact him ASAP. I gather that there is some favourable development. Meanwhile, you may receive a call from INTERPOL Riyadh. Your number has been given to them by Mr Arya.'

Merin looked at the call log on her phone and found that she had missed a call from an unknown number too. She dialled that number.

As the call was picked up, someone spoke broken English in a gentle voice, 'INTERPOL Riyadh. Is there something about which I can help you?'

'Yes please, I am Merin Joseph, Commissioner of Police, Kollam. I have come from India for an extradition. CBI has spoken to an officer in your office. Can I speak to the concerned officer?'

'Yes, it was I who had to contact you. We have in our custody the person you want us to hand over to you.'

Merin was relieved and delighted to get the assurance even though the person at the other end was struggling with the language. 'We will reach your office shortly. Please be ready with all the paperwork and other formalities,' Merin conveyed.

'Please bring all necessary documents and proof of the identities of all the members of your team,' was the request from the INTERPOL officer.

'Sure. We'll be there shortly.'

A little later, Merin called Anuj to tell him that she had been contacted by the INTERPOL office and that her team was about to make its way to get hold of Satheesh. She added, 'Anuj, I don't know how to thank you. The situation was bleak, and I was bracing myself for the worst. The thought of returning empty-handed to India was killing me! I am grateful.'

'Merin, in fact I want to thank you for having brought me into the picture in an act which is going to create history. You are about to get the custody of the first Indian person, accused in India of a heinous crime, to be extradited from Saudi Arabia. I am sure tomorrow the nation will look at your effort with great admiration and awe.'

'Thank you, Anuj,' was the short quip from Merin.

❧

CP Merin Joseph, ACP Anil Kumar and Inspector Prakash were in a cab that would take them to the INTERPOL office. For several minutes, all three were quiet, but their thoughts were vivid and perked-up. Just before leaving from their hotel, they had decided not to talk about the case, and completely avoid any mention of Thakshak Satheesh. They had also decided that if conversation was unavoidable, it should be carried out in Malayalam and no other language.

It was Inspector Prakash who thought he had something important enough to say before arriving at the INTERPOL office. 'Ma'am, I am the IO of the case only in name. The entire work of investigation was carried out by Vidhyadharan and my knowledge of the facts of the case is not as thorough as his,' Inspector Prakash said in Malayalam.

Merin cut him short, 'What's the need to say all this here. We have already addressed it on the flight. We'll talk later.'

'Sorry, Ma'am, I just wanted to clarify…'

'Okay, now keep all this to yourself.'

As they reached the destination and got down from the cab, ACP Kumar paid the cab driver. The latter thanked ACP Kumar in Malayalam and in the same language he conveyed his best wishes to the team for success in whatever they had come for.

As the three cops saw the cab drive away, they looked at one another. Merin and Anil's gazes were fixed on Prakash, the only difference being that one gaze was of utter disapproval, the other was of fury.

As the team entered the Riyadh INTERPOL office, situated in the impressive building of Ministry of Internal Affairs, Merin's thoughts were on what was about to happen. The focused chase she had led was on the verge of a grand finale. The team was escorted to the office of Chief Inspector Abbas. The office presented a picture of functionality. While the interiors, the furniture and the subdued colours and décor were almost banal, one thing that all this conveyed was that the officer who occupied this post was one who prioritized efficiency over flaunting the riches of the state which he served. Sitting across the table from Abbas was Habib, who was introduced to the team. Prakash was the first to greet Habib with a warm handshake. Merin and Anil Kumar exchanged a knowing glance as they saw the new-found confidence of their colleague.

Soon, Merin's thoughts went to the grand spectacle it would be when Thakshak Satheesh appeared and a ceremonial handing over took place. She fantasized that it would be like hitting the winning runs in a packed stadium with spectators on their feet and applauding.

She was disturbed in her thoughts by the matter-of-fact voice of Habib, 'Good afternoon, Commissioner. Before we go for the handing over, let us exchange documents and carry out the rest of the formalities.'

After what Habib had said had been translated by an interpreter, Merin thought of all the trouble she had encountered till then due to the language barrier.

'Good afternoon. Thank you for all the work you have done for us. We really needed to bring the accused to justice, for what he had done was most unpardonable,' Merin replied as papers were exchanged and related protocols followed.

'Routine work, Ma'am. We did struggle a bit to locate the man, but the rest was not challenging.' He smiled and looked at Merin to add, 'Let's go to the hall where we'll hand over the man to you.' He signalled Merin to follow him.

They walked through a corridor and reached an iron door guarded by two armed sentries. As the team reached the door, Abbas signalled one of the guards to unlock it. He did so smartly. They entered the hall and Merin, whose heart was racing at the prospect of resting her gaze on Satheesh for the first time, realized that there was an iron grill which separated the area in which they stood from another grilled enclosure across the hall. The area where they stood was dark, but across the hall, the spot where Satheesh was expected to stand was brightly lit.

Moments later, Thakshak Satheesh was led into the designated area. His downcast head and the hobbling walk displayed the body language of someone who knew there was much trouble ahead for him. Merin had her gaze fixed on Satheesh whose description was well known to her—a slightly built man with a height of not more than 5'3" and a complexion which a lot of men from Kerala had; hardly the big, brawny, thuggish type often imagined when the crime was as serious as Satheesh had committed. He was in the prison uniform used in Saudi Arabia. All these details, however, seemed to be trumped by an ominous change in the atmosphere. Merin's thoughts at that moment of finally seeing Satheesh in the flesh were revolving around the suffering of Pooja and her family. His cuffed hands looked rough and indicated that he was involved in work that demanded using corrosive substances. She winced as she thought of his hands on Pooja's innocent body. For a brief second, Satheesh looked up and made eye contact with Merin. She saw fear in his eyes. She felt a strange sense of relief but not without pangs of guilt for the time it had taken to nab him.

The accused was soon handed over to Merin's team. His belongings—a mobile phone, some cash and documents—were also handed over to them.

As soon as Satheesh came close enough, he started to speak loudly, almost in a shrieking pitch, to say in Malayalam that he was innocent, and that he was being framed. ACP Kumar replied to him with a couple of expletives thrown in, stating that the courts in India would decide his guilt.

Habib asked Merin, 'What was this conversation about?'

'He was saying he was innocent and the officer was explaining to him that the court would decide about that.'

'If I had my way, I would have responded differently. I would have given him a reply which he would have regretted for the rest of his life.' Saying so, he indicated as if such criminals did not deserve civility.

'We have a long procedure to follow. Our courts stick to the laid-down protocols.'

'I must inform you, here in Saudi Arabia this man would be hanged before this month ended.'

Merin tried hard to conceal her disdain at the assertion of instant justice by Habib.

A few minutes later, the teams shook hands.

Soon, Merin and her colleagues were on their way to the King Khalid International Airport after collecting their belongings from the hotel. Apart from an INTERPOL officer, Farouq, they were escorted by a posse of Saudi Police. During this entire time, Satheesh was cooperative and quiet except for a few low-voiced assertions of his innocence.

Their route to the aircraft was so organized that they skipped the various screenings and checks which were routine. They were given a passage through the lounge area and were facilitated in avoiding the other passengers who were boarding the flight. They were also introduced to the pilots and the cabin crew. All this while, Satheesh was in cuffs. He was also subjected to a thorough body search since the usual screening protocols could not be followed. Farouq saw them off at the aircraft to ensure that they were not the only ones guarding the fugitive. They boarded the flight at the very end after all the passengers were seated.

Sweet and Sour

Kochi Airport, Kerala, 17 July 2019

As the aircraft landed, the thud brought Merin back to the present. She immediately looked to the right of the aisle to assure herself that this was not just a dream. There was her prize catch, Thakshak Satheesh, securely flanked by two of her colleagues. She knew she had arrived in her homeland but was unaware of the celebritydom that awaited her.

The flight landed at Kochi airport about 2 in the morning. The formalities at the airport included clearances from immigration authorities. Establishing the identity of Thakshak Satheesh to their satisfaction, attending to the other paperwork related to the red corner notice which was issued by INTERPOL for his arrest, and explaining the reasons for having brought the fugitive in handcuffs were all gone through. It was still very early in the morning, well before daybreak, when Merin and her team along with the accused emerged out of the airport. There, an unexpected surprise awaited them.

Blinding flashlights, video cameras, media persons jostling for favourable spots, questions being asked, all in tandem—with the result that it was all din and no clarity in what was being said. Each one was trying to outshout the other. The decibels were going through the roof. Merin, tired and sleepy only a few minutes ago, was fully alert now, yet not inclined to deal with the media, especially as it was a bunch of highly voluble and clamorous persons. She raised her right hand high in the air like a traffic cop signalling a vehicle to stop. This action made an immediate impact—most of the shouting stopped. ACP Anil Kumar and Inspector Prakash, both dazed by the media frenzy, quickly scurried behind their boss while flanking Satheesh. As Merin continued to hold her hand aloft, the rest of the tumult also gradually subsided.

'As you can see, we have just landed after a journey abroad. It was much of work followed by a long flight. We are here to answer only one or two queries, but please let us go because many formalities remain to be attended to,' Merin announced.

'Madam, congratulations to you and Kerala Police for the successful extradition of Thakshak Satheesh. But we want to know why you have taken up this case on priority? There must be many other cases,' asked the reporter of a national daily.

'I found this case and got to know that this man had been absconding for almost two years. This was a case that had impacted public conscience and people were outraged at the crime. The International Investigation Agency of Kerala Police had been following up with Saudi Police. We just strengthened these efforts,' she explained. 'And I was moved by the plight of a teenager who was so brutally abused.'

'It is said that you took particular interest in this case because it involves a crime against a woman. Is that true?' asked another reporter.

'I must admit that this case touched a chord especially because the victim was a young Dalit girl. I thought that this crime was one which must not go unpunished.' She added, 'Cases related to women and children are close to my heart. I take special interest in solving them. I wanted this person to be brought back to face trial in India. People should not live with the impression that they can commit a grave offence, then escape to a foreign country and evade justice. So the message had to be loud and clear.'

In her answer to another question, she said, 'This was a heinous case where the victim had committed suicide; I felt it was my responsibility to do something about it. Because even though there is a lot of hype around such cases, people forget and move on and that is not fair to the victim, especially to the poor who may not have the resources, and they lose out in the long run.'

'Ma'am, how was the response of the Saudi authorities, and our embassy officials…'

Merin said, 'I must go,' and quickly followed two policemen who made a passage for her past the media clamour.

A few hours later, her name was all over the print and electronic news media. She was overwhelmed to see how her work had attracted attention in the local and national media. She could hardly recognize the dimensions of the fact that she was a celebrity.

One newspaper wrote, 'Merin, one of the youngest IPS officers in Kerala and a vocal proponent of women's rights, earned respect and praise on social media for her determined execution of the investigation.' Some even referred to her as the 'Real Singham'[18]. A channel, *HerZindagi*, headlined the news: 'Meet the Real-Life Singham, Kerala IPS Officer Merin Joseph Who Nabbed Child Rape Accused from Saudi.'

Some members of the media emphasized that the officer who executed the extradition was a young 'woman'. *The Financial Express* of 20 July 2019 captioned the report, 'How a Young Woman Cop Tracked Down a Rape Accused from Kerala to Saudi.'

The news story carried by *India Times* on 18 July 2018 was headlined: 'How This Kerala IPS Officer Cracked a Child Rape Case and Nabbed Accused Hiding in Saudi Arabia.'

Social media went almost hysterical. Posts with pictures of the young IPS officer and praise for her work flooded the channels. Videos of her short career and exploits as a student and officer were all over the media. To Merin,

[18]A fictional police officer in a Bollywood franchise in which the protagonist deals with criminals in a highly exaggerated, dramatic manner.

it was a relief that the reportage was not built around a sexist kernel. It was purely her work as a cop that had grabbed the media attention.

Nobel laureate Kailash Satyarthi called Merin soon after her arrival to congratulate her and wrote a tweet saying, 'India needs more daughters like Merin Joseph in Police. I spoke to her and congratulated for her compassion and determination in performing the duties.'

In the subsequent weeks, despite all the public attention that came her way, Merin displayed rare equanimity and stuck to the facts while speaking to the media. She had quickly learnt to ignore the camera flashlights that now surrounded her every move.

❧

Vinaykumar kept walking towards the blinding lights at the end of the road. He could see nothing around except the dazzle which seemed like it belonged in a celebration. As Vinaykumar got closer, he noticed that a wedding was in progress. Paddy leaves, Pooja's favourites, had been used to decorate the entrance.

'Hello! What took you so long?' the hostess said on seeing Vinaykumar.

'Geetha, what is going on?' Vinaykumar couldn't believe his wife was welcoming him to the function.

'What do you mean? This is no time for jokes. Pooja's wedding is in progress. Don't you have to bless the couple.'

Vinaykumar felt the ground slip from beneath his feet. He ran into the celebration and saw lots of familiar faces among the attendees. He felt like all of them were mocking him with their measured smiles. Frustrated, he moved to the elevated platform where the bride and groom were seated. As he got closer, he noticed that Pooja's clothes were torn. Before he could tap on his daughter's shoulder, the groom turned around and spoke.

'You know what I enjoyed most?' To Vinaykumar's horror, it was Thakshak Satheesh.

'How dare you! I trusted you…'

'Shut up and listen! I really enjoyed tearing her blouse. The fabric being ripped apart was music to my ears.'

'You bastard. I am going to kill you!'

'Hahaha… You can't even touch me. I feel sorry for you, Vinaykumar. You are a loser.'

Vinaykumar suddenly woke up from the nightmare he had had for months now. For him, every minute of knowing that his daughter's violator was back in the country but was yet to face trial, felt like a lifetime. Ever since Pooja had taken her own life, he had slipped into serious depression and despite the efforts of Geetha and their other daughters, he lived with a dreadful sense of guilt. He had stopped socializing altogether, in part due to fear of ostracization by the village community. Even his interest in the case had begun to dwindle as his mental health deteriorated. He would often address either Upasana or Shraddha as Pooja and then profoundly apologize to them.

Vinaykumar looked towards Geetha, who was sleeping peacefully. She had been making futile efforts to keep him optimistic. Due to his condition, she had been at the forefront, helping Kerala Police prepare its case against Satheesh while also running the household. Vinaykumar knew that he had to do better but he did not know how.

As days rolled by, Vinaykumar's nightmares became more vivid, darker. He would often wake up screaming.

Eventually, one morning in July of 2020, as the rain pelted down on Pooja-Shraddha and just a month before the commencement of the trial, Geetha walked into her bedroom to find Vinaykumar lifeless. Upasana and Shraddha rushed into the room on hearing their mother's cries and all three of them tried to pick up Vinaykumar. His body was too heavy and toppled to one side of the bed. The screams of the women were heard by the neighbours who rushed in to help. With the muscle of four people, Vinaykumar was placed inside a van and rushed to the hospital. He was declared dead upon arrival.

At the top of several reforms crying to be made in our criminal justice system is that of speedy trials. Even after Satheesh had been successfully expatriated to India thanks to Merin Joseph and her team's tireless efforts, it took more than a year for the trial to commence. Pooja's already ravaged family had to endure another loss on account of this delay.

Upon his return from Riyadh, additional charges were filed against Thakshak Satheesh by IO Vidhyadharan. The offences incorporated were under Sections 447 (Criminal

Trespass) and 450 (House-Trespass) of the Indian Penal Code and Section 3(a) of the POCSO Act.[19]

The trial of Satheesh in the Fast Track Special Court at Karunagappally took three more years to commence after the initial hearing in 2020. During the trial, the defence lawyers for Satheesh kept harping on his innocence. They even alleged that it was Gopikumar, Pooja's stepfather, who had committed the crime and hanged himself for that reason. A loophole they tried to use to their advantage was the absence of IO Vidhyadharan in Riyadh at the time of the extradition. To have the POCSO charges dropped, it was also contended by the lawyer for the accused that Pooja was not actually a minor. The caste angle was also questioned and the defence argued that the victim was not from a Scheduled Caste. Apart from this, the standard defence lawyer arguments of collusion with the investigating agency and the improper collection of evidence were raised in court.

Salim, the registrar of births and deaths, produced Pooja's birth certificate which read—daughter of Vinaykumar and Geetha Vinaykumar, born on 15.11.1999. Another certificate corroborating the date was produced by the principal of SVHSS Clappana from the admission records of the school. It was thus proved that Pooja had been a minor at the time of the incidents in 2015 and 2016. There was no proof to substantiate the shocking claim that Gopikumar was the actual culprit, and this

---

[19]The Section of POCSO dealing with penetrative sexual assault.

argument was dismissed on face value. As far as the caste angle was concerned, the community certificate of Pooja was presented in court and the *Tahsildar* (tax and revenue officer) who had issued the certificate confirmed its authenticity. The absence of the IO in Riyadh was seen as a mere technical detail which had no bearing on the sentencing of the accused. Overall, the court believed the case of the prosecution.

Thakshak Satheesh was sentenced to ten years of rigorous imprisonment and a fine of one lakh rupees under Section 450 of the Indian Penal Code, ten years of rigorous imprisonment and rupees one lakh under Section 3 read with Section 4 (penetrative sexual assault) of the POCSO Act, five years of rigorous imprisonment and rupees one lakh under Section 9 read with Section 10 (aggravated sexual assault) of the POCSO Act, and imprisonment for life and a fine of rupees one lakh under the SC/ST (POA) Act were imposed by the trial court. He was also found guilty of criminal trespass under Section 447 IPC and under Section 7 read with Section 8 (sexual assault) of the POCSO Act, for which a separate sentence was not deemed necessary.

The court also ruled that if the fine was recovered, two lakh rupees would be awarded to Geetha as compensation.

Several lives were destroyed in the wake of Thakshak

Satheesh's heinous crime. It is difficult to choose the more fortunate—the departed or the ones living in the shadow of unbearable loss. The only silver lining is that the perpetrator was punished in spite of seeking refuge in a foreign land. For that, Merin Joseph and her team deserve all the recognition that has come their way. Their trailblazing action in carrying out the extradition of Satheesh has established a much-needed precedent for other law enforcers to follow.

Preventing a Societal Scar

The true character of a society is revealed in how it treats its children.

—Nelson Mandela

Every child deserves a shield in life which is nothing less than a protracted battle, at times against heavy odds. Child abuse is a societal scar, highlighting society's failures to protect 'the most valuable resource and its best hope for the future.'[20] In fact, such abuse is widespread in measures big and small in all societies.

Child abuse, a shame for any society that considers itself mature and responsible, manifests itself in various forms—physical, emotional, and sexual harm inflicted on minors. The trauma that a child experiences in childhood casts a shadow on the mental and emotional health in adulthood. The wounds of abuse may remain unseen, yet it must be understood that they are usually the deepest.

---

[20]John F. Kennedy, the thirty-fifth President of the United States of America.

Childhood abuse takes away from a person's future the most invaluable gift of innocence.

Society must encourage the victims to share their grief caused by exploitative elders. The fact, however, is that children are told to keep their hurt to themselves. Virtue is seen in the ability of the youngster to remain bottled up and in not revealing the names of the exploiter. The families also force themselves to look the other way.

It has been said that 'in the eyes of a child, silence is the loudest scream of abuse.' In the words of Micere Keels,[21] 'Behaviour is the language of trauma. Children will show you before they tell you that they are in distress.' It is, therefore, the responsibility of society and its lawmakers to establish institutions and laws that can comprehensively respond to the smallest voice coming from the suffering child.

In fact, the conscience of the human race around the world has been pricked since time immemorial. Awareness of the traumas that children have to face in their lives has been the talking point in all societies across the globe. Literature is replete with telling accounts of the tribulations of children and their relentless exploitation by the senior members of society. This led to formulating a Convention on the Rights of the Child adopted by the General Assembly of the United Nations in 1989.

---

[21]Author of *Trauma Responsive De-escalation: Evidence-based Strategies That Work in the Classroom* (2022), *Trauma Responsive Educational Practices: Helping Students Cope and Learn* (2023), among others.

This Convention has prescribed a set of standards to be followed by all State parties in securing the best interests of the child.

The Government of India acceded to the Convention on 11 December 1992. This meant that there was a commitment to undertake all appropriate national, bilateral and multilateral measures to prevent inducement or coercion of a child to engage in any unlawful sexual activity, exploitative use of children in prostitution or other unlawful sexual practices, and exploitative use of children in pornographic performances and materials. In other words, sexual exploitation and sexual abuse of children were recognized as heinous crimes and the urgent need for this to be effectively addressed was acknowledged. The Parliament also felt that it was necessary for the proper development of the child that their right to privacy and confidentiality be protected and respected by every person by all means and through all stages of a judicial process involving the child. Of course, the overarching consideration is that the law operates in a manner that the best interest and well-being of the child are regarded as being of paramount importance at every stage, to ensure the healthy physical, emotional, intellectual and social development of the child.

The above philosophy was the foundation on which the Protection of Children from Sexual Offences Act (POCSO) was passed in the year 2012.

The key features of the POCSO Act are as follows:

- The POCSO Act is gender-neutral. Any gender can be victims/survivors of rape and/or sexual assault under the POCSO Act. A child is defined as any person below the age of eighteen years.
- The definition of sexual offences is broad and not restricted to rape, which is limited to penetration of the penis into the vagina. The Act protects children from offences of sexual assault, sexual harassment, and pornography—for example, penetration by object or touching with sexual intent, or showing pornography to the child.
- The POCSO Act ensures effective access to justice. It entails special procedures for reporting of cases and recording of statements of child victims. It also provides for the establishment of Special Courts for the trial of such offences.
- The POCSO Act makes abetment of, and attempt to commit an, offence against a child punishable.[22]

Government manuals explain that child sexual abuse is a form of abuse in which an adult or older adolescent uses a child for sexual stimulation. Among the forms of child sexual abuse are asking or pressuring a child to engage in sexual activities (regardless of the outcome), indecent exposure (of the genitals, female nipples, etc.)

[22]'POCSO Made Simple'—State Commission for Protection of Child Rights BIHAR.

to a child with intent to gratify their own sexual desires or to intimidate or groom the child, physical sexual contact with a child, or using a child to produce child pornography.

Obligation has been placed on media, studio and photographic facilities to report cases, and the failure to do so has been included as a punishable offence. Likewise, punishment for false complaint or false information has also been included.

The Act has also laid down the procedure for media. No person shall make any report or present comments on any child from any form of media or studio or photographic facilities without having complete and authentic information, which may have the effect of lowering their reputation or infringing upon their privacy. Furthermore, no reports in any media shall disclose the identity of a child including their name, address, photograph, family details, school, neighbourhood or any other particulars which may lead to disclosure of identity of the child, unless such disclosure is found by the competent court in the interest of the child.

The punishments for the offences are strong. There is provision for imprisonment for life (imprisonment for the remainder of natural life of that person who shall also be liable to be fined) for some of the graver offences. Incarceration of ten, seven, five or three years is also prescribed for offences of comparatively lesser magnitude.

∞

In the case of Pooja, the heinousness of the offence led the special court to sentence Thakshak Satheesh to rigorous imprisonment under two different sections of the Act for ten years each, apart from the life sentence he was awarded under the SC/ST Act. Clearly, the trial court was convinced that the offence committed was of serious gravity.

Acknowledgements

After writing about a gruesome crime, it takes a while to find the mind space for penning words of gratitude. But it is a pleasure to acknowledge all those who helped us bring this manuscript together. That helps in clearing the gloom too.

First, to Merin Joseph IPS, who helped us understand not just several aspects of the case but also gave us a glimpse into her early years, we are grateful.

This book has been represented by Suhail Mathur of The Book Bakers Literary Agency. We thank him and his team for getting us a publisher of the calibre of Rupa.

A word of gratitude to our editor, Dibakar Ghosh of Rupa Publications, for giving the book its final shape.

Members of the Kerala Police, CBI and INTERPOL also deserve a special mention for their largely ready assistance.

Appreciation is due for Jacob Punnoose, former DGP of Kerala, who also pitched in.

Our wives, Madhu and Geetanjali, often helped us remain on the same page while writing and, particularly, editing this book.

To our family and friends, we are beholden.